PROTECTING GOD'S GREATEST

*The ABC's of Protecting Your Child
From a Male or Female Sexual Predator*

Judi Davis Tillett

Unless otherwise indicated, all Scripture quotations are taken from the New Kings James and King James Version of the Bible.

Protecting God's Greatest: The ABC's of Protecting Your Child From a Male or Female Sexual Predator
or Female Sexual Predator
ISBN: 978-1-4951-8346-1

In the U.S. write:
Judi Davis Tillett
283 Carmel Valley Way
St. Robert, MO 65584
Email: jtillett@gcccweb.com

Contents

Acknowledgements

My gratitude and love to both Linda Paddock and Kimberly Maskrey for their effort and time with "Protecting God's Greatest." Thank you, dear friends.

My heartfelt thanks to Russ Strand, Hazel Snell, Don Hayden, Glen Waldow, and all the amazing, dedicated people who work to protect children. There are no words big enough but, you do have my prayers. May God bless and anoint every person who works for the protection of children. I pray you all be strengthened to continue and always have His joy set before you. May all your days be lovely and all your nights be safe.

A special gratitude to Dr. Bartlett and Dr. Caro Hatcher. They have both taught and mentored me in God's Way of bringing Light to a darkened soul.

No acknowledgement is complete without mentioning my life long joys, Coke and Ette.

Finally and foremost, my love and devotion to God the Father, God the Word, and God the Holy Spirit. Help us all to yield to Your plan for all the children in "Chloe's world...".

Dedication

for Chloe's World,
and Daniel's,
and Lily's,
and Aiden's,
and Brenna's
and Hosea's,
and Lauren's,
and yes your child,
and for all children,
for they are all God's Innocents and Greatest

The Vision

I was almost asleep when suddenly, I was in the spirit realm. I did not see, but sensed the presence of the Lord. As is often true in spiritual matters there was a "knowing", and I knew the Lord was there to teach me something of extreme importance. I began to see body parts being put together, one leg, one arm, placed and attached to a small torso, until eventually there was the perfectly formed body of a small child. Then it was as if a zoom lens focused in on the head of the child: ears were placed appropriately, followed by nose, mouth, and eyebrows. Then the facial placement stopped. I waited for what seemed to me a long time, and then I said, "Lord, what about the child's eyes?" And He answered, "You are their eyes; they will see what you see". I knew He was speaking to me personally, but there was also an implicit understanding that His Voice and this Vision were to be a shared responsibility for all adults. As I was absorbing this Truth, the eyes of the child were exactly placed. I had time to view the entire, well formed, perfect little person, and then the vision ended.

But also, the vision begins. We are now involved in a great contest for our children. Our responsibility is to instill Godly vision in children and thus help provide security for every child on planet earth.

To those who have been molested, that violation was not, is not, will not ever be, your fault. What innocence the enemy thinks to have stolen, God will restore, and give even more. There is no guilt or shame to the guiltless, to the innocent, and that is you.

Whatever flashes of ugliness the enemy thinks to play in your head
Our God, the Counselor will replace with victory instead
What the enemy meant for bad, Our God will turn to good
And your life and your innocence will shine just as it should
For the Blood of Jesus removes the wound of 'that dark place'

And His amazing Grace obliterates any lie of disgrace
For it is a lie to think it was your fault in any way
And the Spirit of Truth will show your purity and your
  healing day by day
The Light of His glory will show forth in your soul
And your identity will be fully restored and bring His peace
  as you grow

Prologue

She was four years old. She was staring at us with large brown eyes. We learned later that she was appealing to us to see the hell that had become her life. We didn't see. We were her mother, pastor and a police officer. The officer had responded to the child's 911 call. Her mother had been working in the church building from where this little child had placed the call. Her mother, a loving parent, informed us that her daughter had recently spent the night with some friends and the children there had called 911 as a prank. She believed her daughter was simply continuing the play. She wasn't. We missed a call for help and sent her back to the horror her home had become. Her stepfather had been sexually molesting her for months. Law enforcement and social services later discovered that this pedophile was one of the most perverted and heinously inventive "step-daddies" that they in their experience had encountered. She was the tortured victim of his corrupt mind.

This child was loved by her mother and her pastor. But we had not learned to think the unthinkable. This child was vocally mature. This child was also typical in that children lose their voices when they are afraid. She appealed to us in the only way she knew how, and because we were not trained, we missed it.

My intent in writing this is to help save our children from this twisted, demonic, type of hell on earth. My desire is that we see our responsibility as adults and become watchmen and a voice for God's children.

There are ways to die without leaving the planet. When children are sexually molested, portions of their identity alter, close, and sometimes temporarily die. Our job is not to frighten anyone or overstate for drama. The reality of the statistics of child abuse are almost overwhelming and do not need embellishment by any degree. We do need awareness, anointing, and the Body of Christ activated.

This is written for the little brown eyed girl, who is now an adult and that only by the Grace of God. She and her mother are aware that this is being written. It is with their permission and prayer that we share some facts, ideas, and scripture to educate caretaker adults who are committed to protect the innocent. It is with God's love that we understand and share a need to be informed to not just think the unthinkable, but that in so doing, we prevent the preventable.

This is also written with pastors in mind. We hope to help you in protecting your part of The Body of Christ; to help your congregation pray and be an effective part of God's solution against the enemy's plan to destroy generations, one individual child at a time. Pastors especially are aware that there are many children and families ripped, crippled, and sometimes eclipsed by the violent assault of the demonic forces against children. We are increasingly aware that there are many, far too many, children who in varying degrees, are living the hell of the little brown eyed girl. We can and must change this perverted holocaust.

For those who deem it too difficult to think about, please, for a moment, consider the small innocents of God who are forced to live it. I pray you elect to be one who makes a difference for every child you know.

Neither the parent, the pastor, nor the police were dismissive or uncaring of this four-year-old child. We simply were not schooled. We did not know to think the unthinkable to protect this child. We were not awakened or alerted, so we missed the alarm and the appeal. We did not have the education or understanding to seek what we now know is a rising threat against our children. Praise God this child continued to fight for her life and eventually voiced the monster's acts to her mother, who then called me and we acted. Thank God, we acted.

This was not a mother who ignored signs of her child being molested. She simply was not equipped with the information she needed. Her pastor and law enforcement were not uncaring. We just did not know to probe behind the large brown eyes with skill and sensitivity to protect this child who belonged to God.

This book is to raise awareness, equip us, and most importantly help provide protection for our children. This is a book to help us gain solutions. My goal and prayer is that we keep God's children safe in our homes, our churches, and any other environment in which we place them.

The little brown eyed girl is many years later doing well. Not however, without a journey that proves that which bears repeating, that there are many ways to die without leaving the planet.

The mother, after her own daunting journey of pain, is doing well and presently experiences a loving, and essentially healthy relationship with her daughter. This is not a typical outcome and we are beyond grateful.

The stepfather pedophile has since died in prison. During his last conversation with this author, he maintained that he "really had not done such a bad thing" and possibly we all were "making too much of it". This is the pattern and ugly deceit of the self-absorbed child molester.

Let us watch and pray.

"I am only one, but still I am one. I cannot do everything, but still I can do something; and because I cannot do everything, I will not refuse to do something that I can do."   - Helen Keller

Note to Reader

This information is shared in 26 letter format to help you read it in doses! There is some repetition with the hope to produce a more complete understanding from each section.

I am praying for you and your child's increase in vision and victory as your read.

God Bless You — you and your child(ren) matter.

jt

A is for AUTHORITY

"Foolishness is bound up in the heart of a child; but the rod of correction will drive it far from him." - Proverbs 22:15

The word "rod" among other things means "mark of authority". (Strong's Concordance)

Authority is defined as, *"the power to give orders, make decisions, and enforce obedience"*. This definition is also a parental job description. We have been entrusted and assigned by God to *"give loving orders to our children, make decisions for their betterment and maturity, and yes, discipline them toward obedience."* This definition is called "parenting".

(New Oxford American Dictionary)

Parents have the responsibility, under and for God, of shaping the child's will to say, *"yes, Lord"*. Parents are to teach children to be willing and obedient to their Creator and also to their own parental authority. Adults are to train children by teaching them to make Godly choices, a training that should continue as they mature chronologically and as they grow in their understanding of their relationship and purpose with God.

Every child will come to the "age of accountability"; that is, that age, when they will be responsible for their own actions. Paul spoke it well in Romans 7: 9; *"I was alive once without the law, but when the commandment came, sin revived and I died."*

Simply put, there is a time when all individuals will be responsible for what they know, and for what they do with that knowledge. And parents will be responsible for equipping their child to understand the absolute difference between right and wrong choices. If a child is not taught the choice of good as opposed to inappropriate behavior, he or she is left to the devices of worldly input and worldly control.

1

If children are not taught this authoritative and divine order, which forms a secure structure in their lives, they are then more vulnerable to the demonic stealth of darkness and the possible victimization of sexual predators.

It is not only that the untrained child's behaviors are "foolish," but continued foolish behaviors allow the powers of darkness to aim fiery darts at their desired target, which is your child. God's authority plan is purposed for protection. Every child is deserving of that plan. God's Heart of love is the first, the true, and the only pure, child protective service.

This is not to dispel that there are services which must step in and accomplish some betterment for a child when God's real plan is not implemented. Some very caring people work in some of these organizations, and we should be grateful. It is still not the best, ordained plan.

"Foolishness" is defined as "a fountain of foolish actions and impiety." (Strong's Concordance) "Impiety" is defined as "a lack of reverence for God." (New Oxford American Dictionary) That is the definition of the enemies of God. Our job is clear; teach a child to walk under and with the authority of God. We are to walk by faith and teach our children to do the same. We must believe for the "shield of faith" to operate in their lives.

Some would say there are no guarantees of safety for a child. There is, however, the truth and authority of God's Word in which we are to function. The Holy Spirit Himself, will teach us how to train children, how to walk in faith, and the how and why of trusting Him. He is our Helper and our Counselor in the practical application of parenting as well as being our Supernatural Help.

As we instruct our children, the structure of His divine plan unfolds daily in their lives and builds them to sturdy character.

"And Jesus came and spoke to them, saying, "All authority has been given to Me in heaven and on earth."   - Matthew 28:18

"The father of the righteous will greatly rejoice, and he who begets a wise child will delight in him."   - Proverbs 23:24

PRAYER: *Father, we praise You for trusting us to train our children with Your delegated authority. We are grateful for Your Helper and Your truth working in and for us and our children. Thank You for Your 'child protective plan' in Jesus Name. Amen.*

GOD'S AUTHORITY PLAN IS PURPOSED FOR PROTECTION, EVERY CHILD IS DESERVING OF THAT PLAN. GOD'S HEART OF LOVE IS THE FIRST, THE TRUE AND THE ONLY PURE CHILD PROTECTIVE SERVICE.

B is for BULLY

Child molesters are subtle bullies. They are not those bullies who shove, pull, or push in the physical realm. They are doing this in the spiritual and emotional realm and with a very determined strategy. They "groom" their intended victim, and sometimes also the parents of the child.

The following 5 actions of the "Groomer Bully" should be understood as a pattern. The details may vary, but the main intent is to steal your child's affection and to replace your parental, God given authority. Simply put, they want your position in your child's heart and mind.

These bullies "groom" your child with the intent to molest. They actually take dark delight in the game of the grooming process. I have taken the word, GROOM and will use it as an acrostic of sorts to help us recognize and thus prevent their plot.

G ... is for Gifts

The predator will often give gifts to the child to win them over. The child becomes delighted with this attention. Unfortunately, children can be bribed and bought with this sort of cultivation. They can become emotionally connected with the person doing the gifting. They are, after all, children.

Sometimes the gifting is to the parent; it can be tangible or intangible. What candy and toys are to the child, babysitting to give "away time" for the parent can be to the adult. There are numerous "offerings" that may be presented with a hidden motive to disarm child and parent. Often the bully will insert themselves into parental life by understanding you like no one else does. They are empathetic to your needs, and they work deliberately to become a part of your support system.

R... is for Reasoning

The reasoning or motive of the Bully is to remove the authority of the parent and slowly cause the child to rely on the molester and look to him for approval. Subtle. Slow. Certain. Slow is the operative word here. The molester may spend many hours, days, weeks, and months, with you and your child and not expose the real motive. Part of this molester's reasoning is game playing itself, often considering this a sport and wickedly delighting in being the secret master of the rules.

O... is for Override

Override is a word that means to *"be more important than."* Once the authority and reliance starts to shift to the molester, he is able to insert his opinion over the parent. The loving authority of the parent easily becomes, to the child, overridden by a darkening fear of displeasing the molester. The child is becoming groomed to seek approval from the bully. The child often enters the dark place of subtlety as well, and begins to hide the altered allegiance from parental authority.

O ... is for Ownership.

Ownership of the child's emotional structure is the result of the fear and the confusion that the molester has, by stealth designed and planted in the child.

A child may operate from both fear and confusion. The child lacks the understanding of how to assimilate thoughts and feelings and is simply bowing to the predator with his or her behavior. It is to a child, a bewildering bondage.

M ... is for Masking.

Molesters do not have an identifiable appearance. They are skilled at masking. They may look loving, caring, understanding, and even innocent, but behind the mask lurks the predator. A mask is their cover, their disguise. It is worn to hide their amusement at their ghoulish game playing. It is worn to disguise their motive, which is to terrify, manipulate and in varied ways, sexually molest your child. Sadly, the victimized child learns to wear a hiding mask, also.

One area of help with masking is to watch your child's face as you listen to their words. Medical people often speak of inappropriate "affect", which means simply that facial expression does not correspond appropriately with the words being expressed or the situation. If your child masks to a somewhat bland expression when anger, fear, etc. should be displayed, do know this is a learned disguising of emotion and may have roots from a dark source. Explore that!

Watch and Pray. We must determine to watch and pray. We are to be discerning of actions. We are to trust our own spiritual instincts and learn to habitually listen to the Voice of the Holy Spirit.

Again, the stealing of a child's affection and allegiance can be subtle. The blinding process of the parents' need to protect their child from this molester can be subtle as well.

An adult with a right motive to give gifts and offer help should be easily approachable. The right motived person will understand the parents' desire and authority to approve all gifting and the timing of it. It is equally wise to notice if your child has toys, etc. that you did not purchase. Gifts in secret may reveal that a predator has become comfortable with the replacing of your authority. Train your child to ask you before accepting gifts from anyone else.

Parents, verbalize to any adult or teen, a clear understanding that you need to be consulted prior to gift giving. A right motived person, whatever their relationship with the child, will agree and comply. Most adults will already have the concept that alienation of affections and authority is not proper under any circumstances. It is wise to note, mark, and even mistrust the adult who does not respect your wishes. It may just be disrespect (certainly not good or allowable) but it may be more, much more. Always remember, you are the parent, and the person anointed with authority and placed by God over your child. Compliance with your rules requires more than verbal agreement, but also action or in this case, stoppage of action overt or covert.

Important and loving truth: even doting grandparents and other close, involved, relatives need to respect the Godly government of the parents as to the giving of gifts and rule setting.

Does it need to be said that any person, regardless of relationship, who does not respect and follow your guidance needs supervision when with your child? In some cases, you may even need to eliminate visitation. Does it need to be said that parents should investigate whether or not gift giving and cultivating of relationship with your child has ceased? It is necessary to prioritize your child's well being and if that includes supervision or elimination of an adult, just do it.

"Behold, I send you out as sheep in the midst of wolves. Therefore be wise as serpents and harmless (innocent) as doves."
- Matthew 10:16

It is of vital importance to note and understand that we are told to "be wise as serpents" before we are to be "innocent as doves". The wisdom of the serpent is to understand human behaviors. Let us ask God for His wisdom, and watch over our children with it.

PRAYER: Father, I praise you that The Greater One lives in me. I am grateful for the "seeing eye and the hearing ear." You have made both of them, and I "see and hear" so as to bless and protect the children You have placed with me. Thank You, Living God. In Jesus Name. Amen."

8

C is for COUNSEL

What is to be done if you find your child has been sexually molested?

While you will definitely be horrified, angry, and have other converging emotions attempting to overtake you, your priority is your child. Find a place of inner calm, focus on your child and how to best provide the path to healing for him or her.

The first counsel your child will need is the soothing reassurance of your unconditional love. That is the primary step toward healing your child.

It is imperative that you believe your child if he or she has shared the abuse with you. Your child will need to hear with some immediacy from you that, *"this is not your fault,"* and *"you did the right thing in telling me."* This just cannot be overemphasized. Your child must know this and may have to hear it often.

If you found out from someone other than your child, then unconditional love must say, *"I am so glad I found out so that I can help you." "This is not your fault."* For it is not the child's fault.

Do not display panic. You and your child can, and should, sort out other feelings and concerns later. The first consideration is to be a safe harbor for your confused and wounded child. Assure the child of your protection from the abuser. Then assure that protection!

Here is some good counsel of proper procedure:

- Contact the police.
- Call the National Child Abuse Hotline ... 1-800-4ACHILD.
- Do not be deterred or manipulated from exposing the molester

to the proper authorities. If the abuser is also a child, contact the child's parents immediately after ministering to your child.

- Do not allow the accused molester to be anywhere near your child. Set up safety measures at once. If the molester is a family member, remove him or her from your home. Now.
- Do not speak to the accused in front of or within hearing of your child.
- Contact your Pastor or Christian Counselor. Set an urgent appointment. You and your child will need spiritual counseling.

Again, focus on the child's needs. Believe your child, comfort him or her, and assure him or her that they are now safe from the abuser. Your loving, understanding heart and actions are the first comforting counsel toward the healing process.

Parents, you are going to need Christian Counseling to emerge from this. Your child will need a person of Godly understanding to draw him or her a picture of victory, mental health, and an intact identity for the future. You and your child will need someone who knows Christ.

"Counsel in the heart of man is like deep water; but a man of understanding will draw it out."   — Proverbs 20:5

The word, *"draw"* here means *"drawing advice"*. You will need a Godly "drawing out" of the deep things to receive help. Molestation goes deep. Only God, the Holy Spirit, the Great Psychiatrist, can penetrate the depths of the human soul and spirit and with anointing and accuracy redeem what was stolen by the destroyer. Only God through His people can restore the sense of innocence. (Strong's Concordance)

Parents, denial of the assault does not help your child. Thinking that "time will work it out" will not help your child. Taking active steps away from the molester to ensure that it does not continue is indeed correct action, but that is not all the help your child will need.

Do not delude yourself with the thought that children are resilient and that this violation will fade in time. This is not the truth. We are not dealing with a broken toy or a busted friendship here. This is an attack against their personal identity and their present and future relationship with God.

The mirror of who and whose they are has been cracked or shattered. They will need help. So will you.

No matter how traumatic the invasion of the sexual perversion, the Holy Spirit is the Helper and the Healer. He invisibly and powerfully, and often working through His people, takes a trauma and causes a triumph. Time and effort spent toward healing is time and effort well spent.

"If I could relive my life, I would devote my entire ministry to reaching children for God!" Dwight L. Moody, Evangelist

PRAYER: *Father God, thank you for the Gift and Person of the Holy Spirit, Who is our Counselor and Comforter. Lead us Holy Spirit of Truth to the person who You will use to help our child and family through this time. Help us to turn this destruction attempt into a healing and a triumph. We do know that with You there is nothing impossible. We are so grateful that You lead us in a plain path because of our enemies. We follow Your path and yield to Your plan in Jesus Name. Amen.*

D is for DEFINITIONS

Definitions of "typical types" of sexual molestation are more easily understood if we are clear on what is normal and what is abnormal.

Normal is defined as, *"conforming to a standard; usual, typical, or expected"*. (New Oxford American Dictionary)

Abnormal is defined as, *"deviating from what is normal or usual, typically in a way that is undesirable or worrying"*. (New Oxford American Dictionary)

We live in a world with increasingly deviant standards and this produces a mental murkiness to some people regarding what is, and what is not normal in child relationships.

I only wish the following was not a true story. I only wish I had not heard this sort of story, with some variations, many, many, times.

A mother entered her bedroom and saw her husband, her minor son's biological father, putting a condom on her son's penis. The child was approximately 7 years of age. The mother was told that this was dad's way of *"helping his son to understand the need to use protection so that as he grew older he would be sexually responsible"*.

Incredibly to some, mom was uncertain if this was a normal act and pondered it. Out of the confusion and worrying of the encounter she eventually sought help for clarity within her church and family structure.

The seemingly obvious truth is that the condom act was not at all normal, and she was married to a pedophile. The pedophile dad was eventually hot-lined and Child Protection Services got involved. As is usually the case, it was discovered that this perverted act was not dad's first assault against his son. And we do not know how many other innocent children were victimized by this definitely defined pedophile.

No, mom was not of limited intelligence, though that often seems the case to those who hear or read these sick scenarios. The situation does speak to the ability of a molester to cloud and confuse an issue with skillful and cunning words, especially when a person is initially pulverized with viewing the unthinkable. And, of course, the molesters have the power of knowing that we want to believe them, even in the face of the unbelievable.

We must be focused on what is truly normal. It is normal for people of any age to be given respect and dignity regarding their body parts. God wrote that we are to, *"Abstain from all appearance of evil."* (1 Thessalonians 5:22) If we see someone engaged in the "appearance of evil" we are to trust our God and our own understanding.

Normal people respect and teach their children dignity of person. It is not normal for a professing Christian parent to put a condom on his child, of any age, as an act of training in sexual responsibility. It is not normal for a non-Christian parent to do this.

To some this may seem an unnecessary warning. It is not. We have to help people discern abnormal activities in this culture. This particular child could have been spared much if mom had recognized that her husband's other actions were also not normal. She later stated she had dismissed her concerns with her husband's prolonged showering with her son, dad's nudity in front of both her children, and his often preferring to sleep in her son's bed.

If you are a person with concerns, it is wisdom to express those concerns with a trusted family member or church staff who can help you to see balance and truth in what is normal versus abnormal. The world will not be the balance or answer to the definition of normal. The Church must.

Definitions of Predators: a predator is *"one that preys, destroys or devours."*

Pedophile: a sexual pervert in which children are the preferred sexual object. This is not a one-time happenstance. Sexually molesting children is the motive and goal of this perverted person.

Hebophile: a sexual pervert who fixates on pubescent children and would be defined as a pedophile except for the age of preference for his/her fixation.

Rapist: a pervert who unlawfully forces sexual intercourse, usually of a female or a person who is beneath a certain age or incapable of valid consent.

Experimenter:

a) This can be an act with children who are simply curious; i.e. *"show me yours and I'll show you mine."* This is sometimes a part of growing up; parents should not overreact to this. Ask for wisdom and apply it with your own knowledge of your children. You may see a need to discover the source of their curiosity.

b) This can be an older child inappropriately touching a younger child or sexually experimenting with them. This sometimes happens within a family structure. It does not mean that the initiator is a pedophile or has a lifelong commitment to perversion.

Please note that a child molested by an "experimenter" will still need help and counsel. The "experimenter" does also. The "experimenter" may be curious, taking advantage of the availability of a child, or even have a desire to hurt the parents of the molested child. This needs to be clear and calls for insight and counsel.

Stalker: one who pursues quarry or preys on stealthily.

These definitions were taken from *"Child Molesters: A Behavioral Analysis, Fourth Edition September 2001."* There is acknowledgement that even among trained professionals, there is some confusion of terms. For those wishing to develop a further understanding and break-down of these terms, it is suggested this publication be studied.

The "experimenter" definition is from pastoral and chaplaincy experience and training.

These short definitions are to help our understanding, and to help us protect our children. It is important that we do not define childhood experimentation as pedophilia. It is more important that we do not fail to recognize a pedophile or hebophile, who other than the "experimenter" could be defined by all the other definitions, as well.

Law Enforcement endeavors to draw strong lines of these definitions to know how to proceed with appropriate judgement. We should have working definitions so that we may be responsible and proceed with appropriate counsel for the child. Our accurate assessment determines any possible future involvement with the molester.

Children Molesting Children

Anyone with an eye on the news is seeing the reports of children molesting children. This is not a new development; it is just sadly increasing and becoming more public.

Recently a little six-year-old girl was sexually penetrated by an eight-year-old boy. A caring grandmother took her granddaughter to a fast food restaurant. She sat and watched her child in the play area. A large tube-like slide hid her child and the child predator from view. That tube provided the place and it did not take much time for the child to become a victim of sexual abuse. How does this happen in our world? Are we safe anywhere? Rather than cower from this information, I trust we become increasingly diligent and prayerful.

What about that eight-year-old boy? One incident that may help with our understanding involves a six-year-old boy and his four-year-old boy cousin. The six-year-old was discovered performing oral sex on his younger cousin. The boy's parents were seemingly stunned. They were adamant that there was no pornography in their Christian home. They were equally adamant that he had not been molested himself.

There are two avenues that cause a child to act out sexually. They are either viewing a sex act in some form, or it is being committed on them. Sexual molestation acts are not part of early childhood development. If a child is acting out sexually, sex acts have been viewed, have happened to that child, or is happening to that child. Please know this.

Starting with the absoluteness of that truth, we began to unravel the reality of this six year-old's life. The statistics of child abuse caused the first exploration to be in examining his home life. This had to be pursued, softly and without accusation, but it had to be considered. The child is the priority. Caring and innocent parents usually support this.

It was discovered that their neighbors, close friends of the parents, often provided childcare for their son. They trusted the neighbors and it proved out that it was not misplaced trust in them personally. They did, however, have a teenaged nephew who often stayed with them. He was the sexual predator.

Could these boys be described as sex offenders? The answer is *"yes"*. But they might not be defined as pedophiles, yet.

We do need some working definitions as listed so we know how best to apply our help. Christians and Godly counsel are the answer for the child and/or the experimenter. The hard core pedophile is another matter altogether.

There is always hope for any molested-molesting child. That hope must lead to seeking and accepting help to reach a successful life for that child.

Yes, I know this is all hard to read and think about. It is hard to write and think about. And yet, if one child is saved from victimization, it is worth it all, isn't it? We live in that time and season where it is normal to be aware of predators and diligently provide protection for our children.

Not to provide diligent protection in our world, is abnormal.

"Crying is all right in its way while it lasts. But you have to stop sooner or later, and then you still have to decide what to do."
C.S. Lewis, The Silver Chair

PRAYER: *Abba Father, we do love You and seek Your guidance. We will not be that people who "call evil good and good evil". We want to see and assess accurately for the blessing and benefit of our children. Father, we desire to be wise and discerning and thank You that You give us that request. Always, we long to be those people who see and hear what the Holy Spirit is showing and saying to us. Thank you, our Lord for the power and answers of prayer. In Jesus Name. Amen.*

E is for ENEMY PROFILE

"These six things does the Lord hate, yes, seven are an abomination to Him. A proud look, A lying tongue, Hands that shed innocent blood, A heart that devises wicked plans, Feet that are swift in running to evil, A false witness who speaks lies, And one who sows discord among brethren." — Proverbs 6:17-19

This is an accurate description of the enemy, he who is called Satan. It is not a physical description as he is a spirit and a master of disguise. It is a definition of his character and motive. It is significant that his character is described for us in the Book of Proverbs, which was written to give us wisdom for daily living.

Those who follow and are mastered by him are clever at masking, also. Even as Satan can appear as an "angel of light", those motivated by him can appear appealing as well. There is no demonically mastered human who more closely resembles and operates in the attributes of the devil than does the child molester. They are cloaked inside with his character.

An unfortunate fact is that many of us are predisposed to believe that if people look good, and act good, then of course, they must be good. And that, please know, is simply not the case.

This profile of what the "Lord hates" and what is "an abomination to Him", is an inward condition. It is the definition of the devil and his corrupt minions, both his spirit minions and his human ones.

Remember, in this section, we are describing the pedophile and committed molester. To gain and maintain a balance, it is recommended that you view or review the molester definitions.

1. *"A Proud Look."* This "look" has many disguises though mostly is hidden behind feigned humility and manipulative acts of pseudo kindness. Those with a proud look can conceal their arrogance. They can also release it in the features of strong confidence and many people find this form of countenance intimidating and/or even magnetic. It is wise to recall that it was pride that caused Satan's rejection from Heaven.

2. *"A lying tongue."* We have probably all heard the old joke of how to tell if a certain individual is lying, and the answer is, *"if his lips are moving."* Regarding those of evil intent, this is not a joke. Committed pedophiles actually seek out and study truth telling techniques so as to practice and sharpen their skills of deceit. They will lie about small things and large things to inwardly amuse themselves at our gullibility. It makes them feel even more smug and superior. Let us not forget just who the father of lies is and how his spawn also speak.

"You are of your father the devil, and the lusts of your father you will do. He was a murderer from the beginning, and abode not in the truth, because there is no truth in him. When he speaks a lie, he speaks of his own: for he is a liar, and the father of it."
- John 8:44

It should also be noted that many molesters believe or at least want you to believe that they are doing nothing wrong. That falsity actually causes some to see them as wrong but sincerely "nice people."

There are organizations that are attempting to legalize this demonic, lying, philosophy of child sodomy and rape. They call it "love". They declare molestation a benefit to the child as a learning of "love" pathway. It is a way of law now in some countries. It is not "love". It is evil, dark, and the heinous plan of the devil. It is an offense to the Living God.

22

3. *"Hands that shed innocent blood."* There is a cringing reluctance to even share in this area and yet, every thinking, caring, adult will understand the need not to disregard the results of the physical violence done against innocent children. The Word in Leviticus 17:11 teaches that the "life of anything is in the blood." Every violation of the enemy to children, by degree steals some of the life of that child. Sexual perversion and penetration of an innocent child is the enemy's strategy to abort the life of the living. It bears repeating, there are ways to die without leaving this planet, and there are degrees of death.

"Hands" in the Bible, represent power and extension among other things. It is wise to   remember the enemy lusts to reach into your family and in effect extend his demonic hand to destroy and choke out the life that comes from and belongs to God.

We have a High, Holy, and Protective Blood Line. We are to proclaim Jesus' Blood over and for all children. The Blood that Jesus shed is to be proclaimed and spiritually applied for our children.

"And they overcame him by the blood of the Lamb, and by the word of their testimony."   - Revelation 12:11

4. *"A heart that devises wicked plans."* A committed molester is not episodically thinking of evil. It is their constant meditation and motivation. Whatever their outward characteristics, they are inwardly in constant pursuit of victims. Remember again, that they are like their "father, the devil."

"For they sleep not, except they have done mischief; and their sleep is taken away, unless they cause some to fall."
                                                    - Proverbs 4:16

5. *"Feet that be swift in running to mischief."* Mischief is not a cute word. In this sense it means evil. The walk of a predator is ready, running, and constantly seeking to bring ruination. Essentially we are to understand that when a predator sees and/or produces an opening of opportunity to molest, he takes it, and quickly. The word *"swift"* is defined as *"quick and skillful"* and yes, they are. (Strong's Concordance) This does not mean that a predator is not capable of determined and waiting stealth. It does mean that they wait out their opportunity and pounce suddenly. Like a cat with a mouse is the enemy with his prey.

6. *"A false witness that speaks lies."* Those who study the "minds" of pedophiles will tell you that they actually like being accused at times. They take disturbing and horrifying pleasure in "witnessing" their own craftiness in deceit. One need not, nor should we try, to fully understand the dark turns of their filthy mindset. We do need to know the principal plots of their practices. We must be on guard and protective. They enjoy and gleefully employ the "witness" of their words. The enemy's minions are often wordsmiths.

(For those wishing further study on the mindset of sex offenders, we recommend the books of Anna C. Salter, Ph.D.)

Again, the six things the Lord hates describe the devil himself and the interior profile and character of the corrupted humans that the devil owns and motivates.

"He that sows discord among the brethren."

"These six things does the Lord hate, yes, seven are an abomination to Him."

This added seventh, discloses the task of the dark, fallen angel himself. He *"sows discord"*, which is defined as *"strife and confusion"*. And "strife and confusion" are his battleground. Satan is the author of confusion and there has been too much confusion in the battleground of sexual molestation. The "brethren", the Church, must awake and activate. We are to be clear minded and do our part.

Our children are not to be the "ground" of the enemy so that he may "sow" his lies, his darkness and his identity damage. Adults are not to be the cultivated ground where the enemy "sows" his tares while the adult and authoritative keeper of the "ground" sleeps or is deceived.

"For where envying and strife is, there is confusion and every evil work"
- James 3:16

God has described the enemy profile to us so that we will not be ignorant of demonic devices. Wisdom truly is the principal thing. We are to ask, believe, and receive the Wisdom of the Living God. We are called to be effective, spiritually and practically, so as to be triumphant in combat for our children.

PRAYER: *Father God, we ask for and receive Your Wisdom. We are grateful to be people educated and equipped by the Holy Spirit of Truth. Thank you for giving us ears to hear and eyes to see paths of protection and triumph for the Children of the Nations. We effectively resist the sowing of darkness, and we Praise You for a well lit path of safety. We sow Your Seed of overcoming triumph in Your children. Glory to Your Name in and for all generations. Thank you for the overcoming power of The Blood of Jesus Christ, for it is in that Name and Blood that You have provided our victory. In Jesus Name. Amen.*

F is for FORGIVENESS

"And whenever you stand praying, if you have anything against anyone, forgive him, that your Father in heaven, may also forgive you your trespasses."
                                                    - Mark 11:25

How does one forgive a child molester? And why would one want to? The "why" is easier, so we'll start with that.

We forgive because of the powerful truth written in Mark 11:25. God has instructed us that forgiveness is a liberty path that He uses to forgive us. A non-forgiving person develops a hardness of heart and head that will block the merciful pathway of God in all aspects of life.

The Greek word for "forgiveness" in this scripture as defined by Strong's Concordance is:

* *to depart from one and leave him to himself so that all mutual claims are abandoned*
* *to go away leaving something behind*
* *to leave one by not taking him as a companion*
* *Abandon, leave destitute"*

Any of these four definitions describe success to the victimized. To forgive is a freedom from "companioning" with the abuser. Sadly, too many people spend their lives defeated by unforgiveness. For the abused, the act(s) of violence can be their "companion" of defeat all their lives. One does not have to nor should one be, memory-molested daily. That, of course, is the intent of the enemy. He would have a person in the brutal bondage of that molestation daily, hour by hour, minute by minute, second by second, if he could.

The first definition *"to depart from one and leave him to himself so that all mutual claims are abandoned"* is also a definition for divorce. That is exactly what forgiving does. In the "divorcing" produced by forgiveness, the enemy's atrocities then have no future claims to the life of the forgiving person. The victim is no longer "married" to or "coupled" with, the dark pawn of the devil. It is not just small children who must be taught this, but, adults as well.

The "how" is that we forgive by faith, not by feeling. There wonderfully is a place in faith when we can go and abandon the feelings the enemy has evoked. Whether it is the pain of memory, pseudo-guilt, fear, pseudo-shame, etc., the feeling has to be abandoned and left destitute of power. We should not pretend and suppress in our mind the facts of what happened to us. But we can, in Christ's forgiveness, "go away from it and leave it behind."

Only forgiveness can start the production of healing. Small children can be taught this truth. It is for their benefit to forgive. It is vital that we tell the truth to children regarding forgiveness. They are not to pretend. It is a faith confession. They can understand that God has provided a path of forgiveness and that our words with His Word produce change. They can understand and be healed with this information.

Someone wisely said, "Non-forgiveness is like drinking rat poison and waiting for the rat to die." That is a truth.

What a child needs to hear is how forgiveness works. They must be taught to confess-speak forgiveness and then know that their feelings, while they may be conflicting, will eventually harmonize with the Word of God. This is equally true for the adult victim. If your child has been victimized, so have you, and you must forgive as well.

Forgiveness does not produce memory erasure. It does capture, minimize, and eventually cause the incident(s) to fade dramatically in power. We are not saying that memories will not try to erupt and attempt to overpower or even nag at a person. But we are saying that we can diminish, and cast down that power. It has to start with forgiveness.

Forgiveness is for the health of the victim. It is not an open door for the return of the perpetrator. It is not to provide a place of permission to allow the victimizer back into your life and to abuse again. Not ever. We forgive, but we do not give the sexual predator place back into our child's life. Many people have learned this the hard way and often at the expense of a child's safety. Please, do not be one of them.

Forgiveness of an act and a proven life change of the person committing vile acts are not synonyms. Just because we do not drink rat poison does not mean there are no rats.

"Test (prove) all things; hold fast what is good."
- 1 Thessalonians 5:21

Those who deal deeply and often with pedophiles, will share that a proven, repentant life change from a pedophile will be declared by them in this statement, "Do not trust me with children." And we should not.

Molesters are far too often glib in verbal repentance and far too skilled in looking and sounding sincere. This is one of those times where we are providing for children well when we say, "Prove it", and that takes time, lots of time. And distance from the molester, lots of distance.

We remember that the child is our priority. We remember that forgiveness is not a position of possibility to do it again. We remember that forgiveness requires truth, confession, faith, and patience.

The truth is, forgiveness starts healing for the victim. Our confession of forgiveness begins a reducing in the memory of the words and the acts of the enemy. The vision of the mind begins to change from victim to victory.

We have faith in God's Word to begin the quenching of fear and unforgiveness. Faith is how we *"fight the good fight"* to forgive.

(1 Timothy 6:12)

Patience is our path as we repeat our confession of faith and believe for God's Healing.

"The weak can never forgive. Forgiveness is the attribute of the strong." - Mahatma Gandhi

In this statement I agree with Gandhi. We must teach our children to be strong. *"... Let the weak say I am strong."* (Joel 3:10) In all things we agree with God. Confessing forgiveness is a speaking of strength.

PRAYER: *Father, we praise You for the power of forgiveness. We confess we forgive and praise You that You are healing and helping us in our spirit, soul, and body. We have faith in You and the path of Your patience. Thank You, Abba Father that we walk by faith and not our senses. In Jesus Name. Amen.*

G is for GODLY FEAR

Godly Fear is a reverential respect for our Father and this "fear" is a good and holy thing.

The three "fears" below defined are to hopefully eliminate misunderstanding, and to dispel any satanic fear that would wrap us in a shroud of inactivity.

A definition of Godly Fear and it's Godly consequences are written in Ecclesiastes 12:13 in the Amplified Bible.

"All has been heard; the end of the matter is: Fear God (revere and worship Him, knowing that He is) and keep His commandments, for this is the whole of man (the full, original purpose of his creation, the object of God's providence, the root of character, the foundation of all happiness, the adjustment to all inharmonious circumstances and conditions under the sun) and the whole (duty) for every man."

G is for guiding fear. This is a healthy common sense kind of fear. It is also a "sudden awakening" kind of fear that we are on the edge of a dilemma or accident. This fear is exampled in Proverbs 3: 25-26. Guiding Fear is used by our Godly Father and is also a good thing.

G is for guarding against demonic fear. This is a destroying fear that comes from the enemy and produces smallness and limitations. It causes cringing, crippling, and cowardice. It is designed and delivered by the enemy and it is a spiritual torment. It defines who the enemy is and how he operates. Appropriately, he will spend eternity in torment, and an atmosphere of agony that he produced, will be his eternal non-resting place.

Again, the three fears are distinctive. Two are motivations from God and one is the controlling restriction of the enemy. We can discern the difference.

There is no doubt that reading about prevention of sexual molestation of a child, any child, but, especially your child can be daunting. It presents a real challenge. It would be easier not to think about it or not to have to read about it. But ignoring it can be dangerous for our children. We simply have to be informed to be able to take appropriate measures of protection. We must be informed to protect and equip them.

Even as we guard our children we must guard our hearts and minds against the "spirit of fear" kind of fear. We must not be ignorant of the devil's devices. Ignorance is not bliss. It is blistering and brutal.

"For God has not given us a spirit of fear, but of power and of love and of a sound mind." - 2 Timothy 1:7

In any area of guardianship, as with Timothy regarding his flock, there is instruction of what to do and what not to do.

The Holy Spirit speaking through Paul to Timothy reminded him of his responsibilities. He encouraged him to call to mind his gift and his equipping to fulfill his duties.

Parents are called and equipped to carry out God's plan for children. We are to hear, as did Timothy that:

There is a spirit of fear that does not come from God.
God has given us power.
God has given us love.
God has given us a sound (disciplined) mind.

Fear as defined in this scripture is cowardice and timidity. Godly parents have His authoritative attitude that roars forth protection for children like the Lion of the Tribe of Judah. We are not called to be cowards or timid with regard to our children.

We have His power, His defined, "dynamite" power. We are equipped with explosive expression to blast demonic attack into fragmented inabilities. Our spoken words that confess and agree with His Word produce His anointing and His abilities.

A sound mind is a disciplined mind. We must not allow our thoughts to run amuck with dark speculations. We discipline, that is, instruct our minds, to be at peace as we plan for the practical safety and also allow for the supernatural intervention of our Almighty Father God. A sound mind should read, meditate, and act on God's Word, which causes increase in the discerning of good and evil.

Fear that is designed by the enemy is to torment us. Perfect love casts out that kind of fear. We may not be perfect, but, Love is perfected in us by the presence of the Holy Spirit.

"In the multitude of my anxieties within me, Your comforts delight my soul."   - Psalm 94:19

That verse of Truth in Psalm 94 could easily and accurately read, *"Your Comfort, Counsel, Help, Intercession, Advocacy, Strength, and Standby, all those attributes of The Holy Spirit, delight my soul."*

It is imperative that we have this peace residing in us, so that we do not plant fear in our children as we correctly protect them physically and guide them by instruction. The enemy's fear does have torment and can also be transferred. Fear has a face and a feeling. Our children can read and discern both. We should always pray and adjust our face and emotional realm before we share our "safe rules" with our children. Job said, *"For the thing which I greatly feared is come upon me, and that which I was afraid of is come unto me."* (3:25)

It seems that Job is magnifying the power of the world system, the tools of darkness over the One True God. Dark, enemy fear works like a magnet in the realm of the spirit. We are to definitely guard against receiving and transferring it. We must recognize that fear and know that it does not belong to us. We have not been given it by our God and we will not receive it from the god of this world's system.

It is good to remember that while Job did not have a "Mediator" nor that Mediator's Shed Blood; we most certainly do. We are not only to remember that, but we can rely on that.

"Worry is a cycle of inefficient thoughts whirling around a center of fear."   Corrie Ten Boom

That is not us; we have "power, love, and a sound mind." Let's utilize them.

I love the understanding from God of how we are to relate to His Holy Fear in Ecclesiastes 12:13. It is also a *"run to"* prayer tower for us. Let us praise Him in prayer for and with His Word.

PRAYER: *All has been heard. The end of every matter is we reverently fear You, God. We revere and worship You, knowing You and Your goodness. We keep Your commandments, for this is our wholeness, our full original purpose, our reason of creation, the object of Your providence, the root of our character, the foundation of all our happiness, the adjustment to all inharmonious circumstances and conditions under the sun, and it is our whole duty. Lord, we praise You that Holy Fear resists and eliminates that wrong "spirit of fear". In Jesus Name. Amen.*

H is for HOMOSEXUALITY

Over the years I have heard many stories from individuals who have determined that they were homosexual after sexual assault. Some of the reasoning's behind this determination are obvious. Sexual assault attacks the identity.

It is worth noting that Christians are not to be "PC" as in "Politically Correct" but rather to be "PC" in that we are to "Protect Children."

The following information is wording from a letter sent to constituents from Dr. James Dobson's Family Talk. It makes covenant and common sense. Remember that this is the Word View and written and understood from the Christian perspective. The world view is designed to permit - and in our present society to even promote - homosexuality as a lifestyle. We live in a time when the enemy's world system is pushing to produce a mind-set that would make homosexuality not only commonplace, but preferable.

The letter reads in part:

> "... there is no valid scientific evidence to indicate that homosexuality is inherited, despite repeated efforts to find a so-called "gay gene" or other indicators of genetic transmission. If homosexuality were indeed specifically genetic, all identical twins would share that trait, since they have the same chromosomal pattern. Yet, when one twin is homosexual, the probability is only 50 percent that the other will have the same condition. Additionally, if homosexuality were the result of inherited characteristics, it would be "constant" across time. Instead, there have been people groups throughout the ages, such as Sodom and Gomorrah and the ancient Greek and Roman em-

pires, where homosexuality reached epidemic proportions. These cultures and many others gradually tumbled into depravity (as the apostle Paul describes in Romans 1), resulting in sexual perversions of all varieties. Dr. Dobson notes that this ebb and flow within the life cycle of societies runs counter to the predictable way in which biologically inherited characteristics are expressed within the human family.

Furthermore, if homosexuality were genetically transmitted, it would be inevitable, irresistible, and untreatable. Though many individuals and groups work hard to convince the public this is the case, such assertions are simply false. Prevention is effective; change is possible (although often difficult); hope is available; and Jesus Christ is in the business of healing. There is no refuting the fact that countless individuals have left the homosexual lifestyle and found wholeness in their newfound heterosexuality.

Dr. Dobson believes there is a much more verifiable explanation than genetics for the causation of same-sex attraction. It is his view that homosexuality is a disorder that results most commonly from early developmental problems. He feels this is the case despite the denials of professional organizations such as the American Psychiatric Association and their attempts to declare homosexuality as "normal." He is also careful to clarify that homosexual attractions are not typically "chosen." A variety of environmental factors play a role in some individuals, including one or more of the following:

1. serious family dysfunction that wounds and damages the child
2. early sexual abuse

3. the influence of and/or sexual exploitation by an older homosexual during a critical period of adolescence
4. homosexual experimentation, such as mutual masturbatory activity in boys in early adolescence
5. peer rejection or labeling.

There is, of course, a great deal of variance in how these and other forces interplay in individual circumstances."

(Dr. James Dobson, Family Talk, website. Used with permission. Our appreciation and deep gratitude to Dr. Dobson and his staff at Family Talk.)

This is truth. Be encouraged to reread it and be confident in sharing that truth. We must recognize and help children who are struggling with their gender identification. The world view is that we not do this; the God View is that we must.

It is wise to remember that ministry to victimized people of any age does not produce change by demand. We are not called to be repelled by, harsh to, or caustically critical of anyone. We are called, like Jesus, to be touched by the feelings of others. That is what produces the understanding that allows hurting and confused people to yield to the heavenly instruction that produces change.

People desire to change when we reach the core of their damage with the compassionate teaching of our Savior. His Word, the Sword of the Spirit, is anointed and that anointing penetrates into damaged areas of human soul and spirit. Only the Holy Spirit can produce that piercing penetration that heals wounds and causes desire for His best and highest. God, the Holy Spirit pierces the spirit of man and produces a desire in the mind for renewal and a determination to please Almighty God.

Helping people who "believe" that they are other than how God created them requires love, patience, and knowledge as well. It is prudent to study the issue of homosexuality. It is not always as simple as "casting out demons". Though homosexuality is a spirit, it is also a mindset, an identity confusion, and often the result of violent sexual assault.

Most pastors will have studied this issue and be able to provide you with the help needed for success in loving and understanding your child to identity reality. Please, call on them.

PRAYER: *Father, we ask that all Your children be provided with the love that produces Your ordained and genuine sexual identity. We ask and praise You for Your wisdom, knowledge, and understanding. We thank You for our Counselor, the Holy Spirit who teaches and guides us in loving Your people to a healthy and true gender identification. Father, we also praise You for the courage to obey Your Word. In Jesus Name. Amen.*

I is for IDENTITY THEFT

"The thief does not come except to steal, and to kill, and to destroy. I have come that they may have life, and that they may have it more abundantly."   - John 10:10

John 10:10 is a contest scripture. We see that Jesus came because He desires to give us His Life and abundant way of living. The thief, that is the devil, has a threefold objective. He determines to *"steal, kill, and destroy"* God's life in us.

Let us unfold the enemy strategy for clarity and trustingly to prevent his corruption.

   - he manipulates to "steal" our identity.
   - he then "kills" by altering our passion.
   - he then is positioned to "destroy" our purpose.

In this section we will look at his plot for stealing identities. Please read "Z is for Zealous" and "Y is for Your Purpose" for amplification of "kill and destroy."

Matthew 4 teaches that Satan "contested" with Jesus with the intent to cause Him, The Son of God, to be snared by his demonic tools of which there are three. These three comprise the whole world system.

"For all that is in the world- the lust of the flesh, the lust of the eyes, and the pride of life- is not of the Father but is of the world."   - 1 John 2:16

Satan's first pressure point of temptation against Jesus, as evidenced in Matthew 4:3, was to imply reservations regarding His Identity. That was the first fiery dart thrown. If an individual does not know whose they are, then they do not know who they are.

It is this simple to understand. One of the first points of strengthening for any person who has become "born again", a new Christian, is to teach him or her their new Identity in Christ. Once that Truth is established, they begin to grow.

"For you were bought at a price; therefore glorify God in your body and in your spirit, which are God's."   - 1 Corinthians 6:20

"For in him we live, and move, and have our being; as certain also of your own poets have said, For we are also his offspring."
- Acts 17:28

We were "purchased" with the Blood of Christ and we belong to Him. That is whose we are. We belong to God and that knowledge established the foundational truth of our identity. We are God's "purchased", Blood Covenant family and it is in Him that we have our being.

The enemy's threefold world system of tools is sharpened and people are more readily his targets when they have an Identity Crisis.

"Now when the tempter came to Him, he said, "If you are the Son of God, command that these stones become bread." Matthew 4:3 And again, in Matthew 4:6 *"And saith unto Him, If you are the Son of God..."*

Young children belong to God. At their conception in the womb they belong to Him. They are to be taught that truth and to grow up, as His "offspring" into all the covenant passion and purpose of God. So the demonic thief's first point of attack is to steal their identification.

He who was Lucifer is first and foremost an identity thief. He was ejected from heaven as he thought to steal the Identity of The One

True and Only God. He pressed Jesus for His Identity, and he presses against and pursues the identity of God's people and especially His children today. He lost his original identity; he wants the God identity.

To *"steal"* means to *"take away by stealth."* (Strong's Concordance) "Stealth" has the sense of a hungry cat sneaking up to pounce on its prey. And that is how the prowling enemy works.

To destroy a child's identity can be a robbery of long lived consequence. To target and attempt takeover of a child's identity is the enemy's priority as he has then stolen not only the child of God's Love, but His messenger and His message going into a future generation.

We are made by and belong to God. Sexual violations alter dramatically a person's wholeness, well being, and identification.

A person's initial identification is determined in the womb by gender. Typically the first question asked of the pregnant mom or expectant dad is, "Is it a boy or a girl?". There is a seeking of the child's identity by genitalia. The enemy well knows how this works.

Sexual molestations, genitalia violation, often do damage to a person physically and always psychologically. These heinous acts of sexual violation cloud and corrupt human sexual identity. Even as we are initially identified by genitalia, we can be twisted and corrupted by dark manipulation of genitalia.

"When a child is made to participate in a sex act with an adult, it leads to intense feeling of fear and guilt and betrayal, which can easily color his or her entire existence."

(Dr. Keith Ablow — Fox News website)

Far too many ministers and other professionals could accurately testify that the "color" of the molested child's existence often results in gender confusion. The very least of the corrupt "color" is an inability to express their femininity or masculinity in a fully healthy and wholesome way.

There is in a true sense, by the stealing of sexual innocence, a fading away of God ordained wholeness.

Whatever the degree of victimization, i.e. fondling, stroking, penetration, or any form of inappropriate or violent touch, there is always psychological identification damage. The debris left behind can be shame, humiliation, guilt, fear, anger, hate, and usually all of these thoughts and feelings. They are the stunting devices, the tools, of the enemy.

These tools of the enemy's trade often grow to increasingly overwhelm the victim and result in acting out in various forms of anger. That anger sadly, fuels many victims to perpetuate the cycle of violence and take on the role of their predator. They take on the role of identification assassins. This is the enemy's ultimate plan, to "steal, kill, and destroy" generations.

Understanding the damage caused by sex sin is necessary to partnering with God in protection of the innocent. The understanding of that damage is also necessary in the restorative healing process for those who have been violated.

It is important that we know that no child, actually any person who is sexually violated against his or her will has lost their purity. But, sadly, they have had their innocence stolen, and their identification is in jeopardy.

"The true identity theft is not financial. It's not in cyberspace. It's spiritual. It's been taken." (Stephen Covey, Brainy Quotes)

"It is only because He became like us that we can become like Him."   Dietrich Bonhoeffer, The Cost of Discipleship

Thank you, Mr. Bonhoeffer, for that is exactly our identification process.

PRAYER: *Father, we thank You and are grateful that Your life defines ours. You have formed us in the womb with the intent that we identify with and imitate You. Whatever the enemy thinks to have stolen, we know that You restore us to health and rightful position. We belong to You and we will walk in Blood Covenant innocence by Your grace and sufficiency. You are, in all things, more than enough. The enemy is defeated and we are defined by You and Your Word. We walk in Your Word and identify with Your Truth. In Jesus Name. Amen.*

J is for JESUS DREAM

It would seem unconscionable to write about the protection of children and not mention the murderous darkness of abortion.

Since the *Roe v Wade* decision in 1973, there have been over 1,323,604,512 abortions in God's World. As you are reading this the numbers are increasing. It will hopefully cause an igniting of passion for Life to google one of the abortion clock counters and watch the slaughter of children designated by numbers, alarmingly increased second by second as you watch. Horrifying, but we must believe that it is still stoppable.

Let us remember that the *Roe v Wade* decision was based on a lie. Jane Roe declared she was raped and later shared that she had lied. That "lie" has become a "legal murder" devised by the "father of lies and he who was a murderer from the beginning."

"You are of your father the devil, and the desire of your father you want to do. He was a murderer from the beginning, and does not stand in the truth, because there is no truth in him. When he speaks a lie, he speaks from his own resources, for he is a liar and the father of it."   - John 8:44

This scripture sums up the original abortionist.

It is true that there have been recent closings of some abortion clinics. That is good news. Whatever those closings are due to the morning after pill, better birth control methods, abstinence, or hopefully the prayers of the saints, it is still not enough. We must passionately care and fight this in prayer, and win. Really win.

The motive for murdering these babies in the womb, whether partially birthed, or fully birthed, is clearly defined in Psalm 139:13-16.

"For You formed my inward parts; You covered me in my mother's womb. I will praise You, for I am fearfully and wonderfully made; Marvelous are Your works, And that my soul knows very well. My frame was not hidden from You, When I was made in secret, And skillfully wrought in the lowest parts of the earth. Your eyes saw my substance, being yet unformed. And in Your book they all were written, The days fashioned for me, When as yet there were none of them."

As we read those verses, it is clear that before a child is born, God has "fashioned his days". That means He has pre-ordained the path of each life and placed His plan of divine activity in each one.

Christians are aware that babies are alive, feel pain, and are real people in the womb. That life starts at conception. That is fact. It has taken science a while but technology now allows a fuller understanding of life in the womb. Realities recently "discovered" show that babies in the womb experience Rapid Eye Movement (REM), which we know indicates dreaming. Babies in the womb experience dreams.

Obviously, womb children are not dreaming about the playground they visited yesterday or longingly dreaming to visit again. It is no stretch to our thinking, based on Psalm 139 and other scriptures, that God is pouring His Vision for their lives into their little, yet alive, spirits.

There is no way to commit to protecting children without mentioning our great need to pray against abortion, which is murder. We must pray and then activate in a stand for Life. The Life of God breathed into all children indeed matters. With the entry of His breath, is the entry of His dream. We are to "open our mouth for those who cannot speak for themselves."

"Open your mouth for the speechless, in the cause of all who are appointed to die."   - Proverbs 31:8

The enemy of God must be stopped from his killing of the innocent. These womb children house dreams that Jesus has provided for them. They are alive with great, holy, and anointed adventures that God has prepared.

The father of lies knows this truth quite well. And his plan is to kill the "Dreams of Jesus" before they have time to bear fruit. The devil knows of life and dreams in the womb. The Body of Christ must know this. We must activate in the natural and supernatural to stop abortion. Again, the devil knows he is aborting the people and the plan of God on earth. The people of God must not be ignorant or indifferent or overwhelmed with abortion, what it is, or how large a killing place the womb has become for the devil.

"If a mother can kill her own child what is left for me to kill you and you to kill me? There is nothing between."   Mother Teresa

There is always the concern that those who have committed abortion do not know that they can be forgiven. Forgiveness is yours for the asking, when there is genuine repentance. And we praise God with and for anyone who repents. We rejoice for the healing from Heaven that our God gives.

Please know that the prayer of mercy will need to be applied to the "seed father" as well as the "womb mother" of aborted children. Often the accountability of aborting children is applied to the female only. Every male and female is accountable to God for beginning or ending His path of Life and His plan of divine activity in a child. It is a fool who thinks that he may "spill their seed" and not be as accountable as the female who houses that seed of life.

47

Again, before mercy can be applied there must be repentance. We do praise God that His mercies are new every morning, for those who seek it and apply it.

"There can be no keener revelation of a society's soul than the way in which it treats its children."

Nelson Mandela, former president of South Africa

I would add to this truth that there can be no "keener revelation" of a Christian's soul than the way in which he or she treats children. How we respect God's Life at any of its stages declares who we are and what we actually believe and value.

PRAYER: *Father, we ask for your help in stopping the aborting of Life. We breathe in and take fresh breathe of Your dreams for us. We desire to be Your Voice and Your Hands on this planet. We take authority for children in all stages of Life. Abba Father, may Your Dreams truly come to fruition on this planet called earth. We love you, Living God. We love and care for every child You create and we open our mouth for those unable to speak for themselves. We genuinely repent of those things we have not done, and we now take prayer responsive action. Open our eyes that we may see what to do and where to do it. Help us to minister mercy to those who through ignorance, indifference or confusion have been life and dream murderers. We take authority for Your plan of Life. We speak and act with Your Anointing that will break this horrific yoke of bondage. In Jesus Name. Amen.*

K is for Four KINDS of Love

There are four Greek words for love. These words have been historically difficult to separate for definition, but, in our culture they have been separated and defined for understanding and application.

It is crucial to have a working knowledge of these definitions for clarity in a confusing world system. The world system tosses out the word "love" in a determined attempt to cause conflict and drain our sense of true understanding and distort authentic compassion.

Far too large a portion of God's Church has lost and/or abused these definitions and that has resulted in some Christians becoming blended into the dark fabric of the enemy's system of thinking.

The truth of love, when not authentically defined, leaves an open playing field for Satan and his minions, be they his demonic spirits or his deceived and deceiving human following.

Agape:

Agape is used by Christians to express the unconditional love of God. This word means love in a spiritual sense. It is selfless in that it gives completely and expects nothing in return. This kind of love is about sacrifice. This love sees flaws and human failures, but is absolutely not moved by them. This is the God kind of love. God does not have this kind of love; He is this love.

Romans 5:5 teaches us that this love is *"shed"* or poured, distributed, into our spirits by the Holy Spirit. This love that enters into us by The Holy Spirit gives us the amazing ability to love like God Himself. It is His Love in us flowing through and from us.

Phileo (Philia):

This word of love references a warm, affectionate, platonic, friendship love. It denotes commitment to a person that you choose to love. For example, you may have an agape love for your enemies, but we are not required to have a phileo love for them. This love is a give and take love. It includes loyalty to friends, family, and community. It requires virtue, equality, and familiarity. Again, phileo is a choice or 'mental' love of the will.

Storge:

This is a family and friendship love. It can be described as the natural love parents feel for their children. It is also the love of family members and chosen friends. Storge love accepts flaws, faults, and is the love that leads us to forgive. It is the love that makes us feel safe, comfortable and secure.

Eros:

Eros is defined as romantic and sexual love. It is passionate and intense and arouses strong feelings of desire toward another person. However, it focuses more on self than the person desired. This is an important emotion, and especially in the beginning of relationships.

Like all genuine love, this was created by God and designed by Him to produce a sex life of enjoyment and fruitfulness for a man and a woman who have entered into His Covenant of Marriage. For this love to last, it must be moved to a higher level; that is away from self and toward the marriage partner.

This love provokes strong sensual desire and longing. It is generally pure emotion without the balance of logic. The power of this love should be obvious. An understanding of its definition helps us to see why we need to learn and live the other three. Eros must be cultivated, calmed, and should never be the love that leads our decision making. Agape should be the Love that leads and governs the phileo, storge, and eros loves.

The enemy and his followers are absolutely incapable of Agape, phileo, or storge. God is the Agape that is also Light, and in Him is no darkness at all. The enemy is dark and in him is no Agape or Light at all; he can appear as light briefly, but there is no quality substance in that appearance. His appearance could be illustrated as like a chocolate covered spider, full of poison but, appearing desirable. Only the fire of God's Spirit can produce the heat and the melting so that the 'hair' and the venomous intent emerge.

What the devil has been able to achieve through various forms of media is to magnify eros to the exclusion of Godly government, logic, or common sense. Without God governing eros, it stands for self and self alone. Eros ungoverned is the path to a narcissistic, hedonistic, and perverted lifestyle.

Eros, without the government and Covenant of God becomes in the hand of the enemy, like that chocolate covered spider. Again, the enemy has used the media effectively as a tool to achieve an onslaught and often effective, self-serving and self-deserving, pornographic weapon. What we pay attention to is what we desire. This is one major reason God says, "pay attention to my Word". The Word is the fire that melts the chocolate facade.

Consider this, Satan was ejected from Heaven as he wanted others to worship him as he worships himself. On planet Earth he has developed a world system comprised entirely of *"lust of the flesh - lust of the eyes - pride of life"*; three self-centered, totally hedonistic character traits. 1 John 2:16

Now consider also the pedophiles: everything they think and do is all about them and their lusts. They are self-centered and their total desire is to delight and fulfill themselves. The objects of their lusts, children, are to them, just that, objects. They have no Agape (capitalized so we remember this is the God Love), no phileo, or storge. They are entirely triggered by ungoverned eros.

There are groups now actively lobbying for "pedophile love". The following are a few statements from the Paedophile Information Exchange (PIE):

> *"Where both partners are aged 10 or over, but under 14, a consenting sexual act should not be an offence. As the age of consent is arbitrary, we propose an overlap of two years on either side of 14."*

> *"Childhood sexual experiences, willingly engaged in, with an adult result in no identifiable damage."*

> *"The Criminal Law Commission should be prepared to accept the evidence from follow-up research on child 'victims' which show there is little subsequent effect after a child has been 'molested'."*

"The present legal penalties are too high and reinforce the misinformation and prejudice ... against child sex offenders." Extracts from an National Council for Civil Liberties (NCCL) report written for the Criminal Law Revision Committee

These "views" are straight from the father of lies. This is but a small sampling of the turn of some so-called fact finding organizations that are determined to legalize child molestation. Even a casual study of the damage done to a child, and yes, age 14 is a child, shows the extreme destruction produced by sexual assault.

There is no "pedophile love". There is pedophile lust called eros. Every Christian and thinking person should be aware that the enemy is driven and determined to legalize child molestation. We must be awake and pray. We must recognize demonic intent and not allow this spiritual wickedness from demonic high places to succeed.

Recently the American Family Association, shared an announcement made by the American Psychological Association (APA). In its latest edition of the Diagnostic and Statistical Manual of Mental Disorders the APA states it now classifies pedophilia as a sexual orientation or preference instead of a disorder. (Charisma News July, 2015)

It is not difficult to see what the enemy of God plans to do with this redefinition. Evil desires to reshape our thinking, and produce an easier, even acceptable, path of darkness to make children his prey. We do not have to yield to his terms. Let us determine to know that God defines this as child molestation and abomination, and we fight the good fight against it. It is not a "preference or disorder" it is a perversion; a sexual perversion straight from the depths of darkness.

The twisting of words will not change the truth. I trust our God that the devil's definitions will in no wise deter the actions of His Body to stand firm against sexual perversion.

Only God is Love and He is not in favor of, indeed is adamantly opposed, to child molestation.

We must use our voices in prayer and take authority with knowledge and wisdom. We can and must win against this venomous spider and his attempt at legal webbing.

Please read Dr. Keith Ablow's article in the Appendix section. It will aide in understanding how the enemy of Life and God's children is attempting to drive his agenda, not only to allowance of their perverted behavior, but to produce protection and provision for them by the government. We simply cannot sleep through this demonic push for perversion. We must stand against this and for God. Our enemy is relentless. We must be vigilant.

PRAYER: *God's Love is poured into our hearts and we thank You for that, Holy Spirit. We will not be indifferent nor blinded by the enemy tactics of confusing definitions. Thank You for Love's vision and victory. We have spiritual eyes to see and we praise You for teaching us, leading, us and guiding us into all truth. Father, we are ever mindful and alerted to the destructive plan of the enemy. We trust, act, and rest in the Anointing that breaks bondage and sets captives free from enemy devices. Lord, no matter how loud the corrupt culture shouts, no matter how large their numbers, we stand in victory for Your innocent children. When the enemy declares by so-called legal gains, that molesting children is acceptable, we stand and speak with the Fire of Your Truth that burns away the dross of lies. We will be diligent in every season and for every child. In Jesus name. Amen.*

L is for a LIST of SAFE PEOPLE

Children can, and should be, taught at an early age about their body parts and their right to privacy. They should be taught who may touch their private parts. This is providing protection for your child before the enemy slithers in with confusion and physical assault. Your protection in place provides resistance to the plan of the predator.

As your child is being trained on the potty is a quality time to provide them with a safety list. That is, a list of people that you have determined may bathe them, take them potty, see them naked or experience their nudity for any reason. Potty training, yes, that early.

You could possibly start with a fun story or verbalize some of the many ways they are important to you. They will definitely enjoy the attention and that gains their listening.

Sit on the floor and use your "eye level" connection to share that God made them and that they are wonderfully made. Begin to share with them the wonderful parts that God made private. Name those parts.

It is always wise to use anatomically correct words with even the smallest child. This is a major way to teach them to communicate accurately. We all would like to believe that nothing sexually perverse will ever happen; nonetheless, every child should be equipped with a descriptive vocabulary. They need the right words to be able to communicate effectively. Far too often little children are minimized or dismissed because they are not equipped to share what actually happened.

Drawing pictures or marking areas on anatomical silhouettes may work well for children but is not always effective if they should ever need to be under examination. An accurate vocabulary can spare a child continued and increased abuse, or prevent them from being disregarded as fantasizing or even coached to erroneously accuse someone of sexual misconduct.

Unfortunately, this does occur. Sometimes in the case of acrimonious divorce, an angry parent will exploit his or her own child for selfish benefit. That is detestable, and an issue that deserves teaching about and against. Our focus, however, is on equipping our children with proper words to communicate effectively for their safety and benefit.

Potty training examples:

"Alice (or John), God, Who loves you even more than Mommy, made your vagina (penis) body part. It is this part (point or touch softly). This part of you may be touched by Mommy as I help you with potty and with bathing. The only other people who may touch you are Grandmother and Aunt Betty (Grandfather and Uncle Michael). They will help you sometimes also because I give them permission. If any one else ever tries to touch you, you must tell Mommy. Do you understand? Now, WHO can touch your private parts, your vagina (penis)?"

As they repeat the short and safe list, encourage them that they are really special for remembering the list. They are. And so are you, for equipping your child.

Keep it light and in a loving, fun, voice. This will bear repeating as your children grow. There is no magic number on how often to repeat this routine, but it must be sown into your child's soul.

Obviously, it is imperative that your safe list be truly safe. If the list for any reason changes, relatives moving, deaths, etc., make sure your child is aware of a new list and why it changed. Always emphasize, that your great, good, job is to "keep them safe and

56

happy."

Other than the help to potty, bathe, etc. that may be provided by both biological parents; it is usually wise to have your safe list determined by gender.

As your child matures in understanding, you should also share that if they feel uncomfortable when anyone touches them on any part of their body, they should tell you. It needs to be stated that a pedophile can molest and experience physical stimulation and sexual release by a lingering touch or stroking any part of a child's body. This is where we learn to trust our child's instincts and our own. Sometimes a child's loudest cry for help can be an appealing look toward his or her parent. Even if it is, or seems to be, an innocent physical contact and the child does not like it, respond to the need/desire of the child. This response on your part builds an awareness in your child that you are indeed his or her protector.

Repeat: *"Alice, who may touch your vagina or see your body parts? It is important to remember so I can keep you safe and happy. You are so important to God and to me."*

Pray that God enlighten you in developing you short and safe list. Trust Him. Trust yourself. Trust your child.

Ask yourself:

1. What is my personal history with this person?
2. Would I trust him or her with my life?
3. Do I experience intimidation often from him or her?
4. Does he or she love me?
5. Does he or she show respect and yield to my decision for my child even if we disagree on some minor child development matters?
6. Does he or she show genuine love for the child for whom I

would give my life?

Do not assume that teachers and pastors, simply by their position, are trustworthy list people. Even casual readings of the news would declare that those who should be are not automatically "safe people" in this age.

90% of child victims know their offender, with almost half of the offenders being a family member. Of sexual assaults against people age 12 and up, approximately 80% of the victims know the offender. (Megan's Law - Office of Attorney General)

This data continues to rise. We must equip our children without imparting the wrong kind of fear.

Children simply trust adults, especially the ones with which they see you relating, laughing, and hugging. The following illustration may help to shield your child against family member assault.

Pick a time to sit with your child in view of a tree. Talk about the tree that God made and the many branches displayed. Share how fun it is to climb trees and that you perhaps enjoyed that activity as a child. Then explain that some of the branches may look safe to climb but they are not as they are not sturdy or have other hidden danger. Make sure they understand that an unsafe branch can cause pain that results from scrapes, cuts, or broken arms or legs. Explain that sometimes because some branches look safe, we disregard good safety rules. Enforce the thought that tree branches need to be tested for safety.

Share that as they grow there may be times when you are not there to guide them or that you may misjudge the safety of a branch yourself. Do let them know that you are always available if they are hurt in any way because a tree branch proves not to be safe.

Once they comprehend that, then share softly, calmly, that some-

58

times families are like trees, in fact, "family tree" is a commonly used term to define families. Tell them that, "sometimes people are like tree branches. Some may look safe, but they are not. We just do not always know if they are safe, that like some tree branches, there can be hidden danger."

Share that it is disappointing when people do not prove to be safe. That sometimes trusting the unsafe people causes pain like falling from a tree branch or scrapping a knee.

Reinforce your relationship. Tell them that, "but, you have me and you can trust me. I am here to help you. And I have you, and I trust you. We have each other. I love you and I know you love me. We can share and prove things together."

Then just wait. Be patient. If there is something a child wants to ask or tell you this may be a paved moment. You may wish to refer back to "A is for Authority" and remind your child that God has instructed you to "keep them safe and happy".

This time may also provoke questions you are not prepared to answer about some other family matter. *"I don't know"* is a good answer sometimes.

Be very certain to listen carefully to anything they may say. They may say, *"Well, brother is not safe, he hits me sometimes"*. Listen and share that while that is not right, there are solutions. Give them solutions. If a child is being molested, this solution may be the path to the next solution of that exposed "unsafe branch."

Keep it simple. Keep it fun. Perhaps climb part of the tree and practice some safety rules. That makes a lasting impression.
"And he shall be like a tree
Planted by the rivers of water
That brings forth its fruit in its season
Whose leaf also shall not wither

And what ever he does shall prosper." - Psalm 1:3
The Word makes a lasting impression. Share this scripture as well.

No one knows your child's readiness to learn and comprehension level as well as you. You may have better illustrations than the one above. Good, just share it and keep dialogue open. That 90% statistic should loom large in our protective thinking.

"Tell me and I forget, teach me and I may remember, involve me and I learn."   Benjamin Franklin

That safety list, that family tree illustration, that is involvement.

PRAYER: *Father, we praise You that You show us who the safe people are for our child's protection. We know Your Heart and desire for this child You have entrusted to us. We determine to pray and to hear and obey Your Voice. We praise Your Name as we wait upon You for instruction regarding our child's safe list. We yield to Your softest check in our spirit as we seek guidance to discover those You have provided to love and protect this child. We praise You for Your goodness and for the truth that absolutely nothing can be hidden from You. We love You. We trust You. In Jesus Name. Amen.*

M is for MESSENGERS of Moral Courage

"You shall teach them diligently to your children, and shall talk of them when you sit in your house, when you walk by the way, when you lie down, and when you rise up."   - Deuteronomy 6:7

There is no doubt that we are all called to teach and train our children in the covenant ways and commands of God. And there is no doubt that we will need to protect them so that they may receive the message of God.

Each generation is called to instill God's message to the heart and mind of the successive generation. That will require protecting the next generation, not just by teaching the message, but protecting the next messengers, our children.

The enemy does know that time is short. But what does that mean to him, an eternal spirit who cannot receive the truth? He can speak facts and distort the truth and his desire is to stop the message of God to the next generation, which means he plots to stop the next generation from trusting God. He can and must be overwhelmed and halted by the authority given to the Church by God.

To win the war for our children, the Church must lead the way in "moral courage" and not idly hope that someone else takes care of this matter. It should be obvious to us that the elusive "theys" of this world are not protecting our children. We, are the hope, the soldiers, for the innocents who all belong to the Living God.

"You therefore must endure hardship as a good soldier of Jesus Christ."   - 2 Timothy 2:3

The word *"hardship"* simply means to *"endure the hardness of military service."* For God's adult soldiers, we must have moral courage to be good soldiers in the army of the Living God. (Strong's Concordance)

Please read carefully the following article published by Dr. Keith Ablow in 2011. He addresses the infamous pedophile Jerry Sandusky case. He points out that people, especially Coach Joe Paterno, who though aware of Sandusky's deviant behavior, did nothing.

What Joe Paterno Could Have Prevented

According to recent reports (including his own), Joe Paterno, the legendary football coach at Penn State, knew back in 2002 that his defensive coordinator, Jerry Sandusky, was an alleged pedophile who had sexually assaulted at least one young boy. Yet, Mr. Paterno did no more than report the incident to other administrators at Penn State, while continuing to work alongside Sandusky.

Now, Sandusky has been charged with sexually abusing eight victims, and there well may be more.

Mr. Paterno has stated that he is devastated by these events and wished he had done more to prevent them. I wonder, however, whether he has a real understanding of exactly what injuries - from a psychological standpoint - he could have prevented.

As someone who has treated victims of sexual abuse over the past two decades, I could tell him. He could have prevented catastrophic dynamics from unfolding in the lives of victims and their families.

When a child is made to participate in a sex act with an adult, it leads to intense feelings of fear and guilt and betrayal, which can easily color his or her entire existence.

These feelings are often suppressed. Hence, they can crop up in devastating ways later on: in an inability to trust any authority figure, in a tendency to avoid feelings at all, in literally slipping away from reality (dissociating), in attempts to suppress memories and feelings using alcohol and illicit drugs, in attention deficit disorder, in major depression, in sexual disorders and in suicide.

The key understanding why so much and such severe psychological fallout can attend sexual abuse is that children are simply not equipped emotionally to participate in a romantic or erotic relationship with an adult. Therefore, they are, by definition, being overwhelmed and commandeered for the gratification of a much more powerful individual. They are, for all intent and purposes, being psychologically kidnapped, with all the related feelings of powerlessness and impending doom. And for those who cover up those feelings by pretending to have been favored by their abusers, there is always a day of reckoning with the reality that they were only the favorite victims.

Mr. Paterno may have known what it took to win on a football field. He may have known something about courage when facing big men running full tilt toward you, intent on stopping you, but he apparently knew nothing about moral courage, nor how to protect those among us who really need protection. It's time that we made that distinction plain. And this is a case in which it could not be plainer."   *- Dr. Keith Ablow*

Note: those who study pedophilia and the predators themselves, will tell you that the "average" molester will have committed over

360 assaults before caught. Not the number of victims usually, but the number of times they have sexually victimized.

Dr. Ablow's article is insightful and powerful. It is a teaching tool. It is also a clear call of protective responsibility to every adult, especially those of us who profess to follow Christ and His teachings.

Reading Dr. Ablow's statements along with our Biblical understanding we know again the why of Satan's determination to molest; it produces "distrust of authority and to desert one whom he ought to obey".

We, The Church, must not be in the position of "wishing we had done more". The ascending numbers of molested children make a clear and divine demand on us to become proactive now.

We have no desire to add injury or pain to Mr. Paterno's family or to focus solely on him. However, we do have an obligation to the Spirit that resides within us to be more than "just devastated by these events." We should not just "work alongside" destroyers of children. We should be sounding a long and loud alarm about and against them.

In our schools, parks, homes, and yes, even in our churches, this insidious destruction increases. Could that increase partly be a reflection of a prevalent tendency to protect the child molester instead of the child? We must not protect the pedophile. We must not.

We must be messengers of moral courage. We must.

"Children are the living messages we send to a time we will not see."   John W. Whitehead, founder, Rutherford Institute

That statement by Mr. Whitehead is a great Truth and our God's plan.

PRAYER: *Father, we pray for eyes of discernment as we set a watch over our children. We are strong in You and in the power of Your Might. Yes, we are strong and very courageous as we see Your prioritizing of children. We are bold and we take an irreversible stand to protect the innocent and expose the predator. You have set our course, and our face is set like a flint to do the right and good thing. We determine to glorify Your Name in all the earth in every generation. In Jesus Name. Amen.*

N is for NICE

Private behavior canNOT be predicted by public behavior.
Private behavior canNOT be predicted by public behavior.
Private behavior canNOT be predicted by public behavior.

Repeated on purpose as that cannot be said enough and it cannot be overstated.

Nice is a honed social skill, not a fruit of the spirit. (Galatians 5:22)

Nice can be defined as *"pleasant and agreeable"*. There are predators who practice and pride themselves on appearing and acting "nice."

There is a true case study of a clean cut, young man who was a youth minister. He dedicated himself to the appearance of "nice." He mowed the lawns of the senior citizens at his church. He provided part of his salary to help feed and provide for the poor in his community. He baby sat and ran errands for the families in his church. He displayed good manners and respect to all in the congregation. And all the while he waited, he lurked, he kept his "chocolate covered spider" facade away from any heat of discovery.

During this time he also ingratiated himself to the children in the church, specifically those who were defined as "at risk" children. He began, after his dark waiting period to sexually molest those children. Who really believes "at risk" youngsters anyway? Some were too afraid to tell and those who tried were dismissed as "we all know children lie" and especially those who have been labeled "at risk." If there were any questions put to him regarding accusations, the church staff met and of course, concluded that these accusations are part of the enemy's plot to discredit the ministers of God. Any apparent evidence was eclipsed by this predators "niceness."

This particular pedophile then began the grooming process of other children in the church. Without consequences, the predators are emboldened with their own ego and insatiable lusts. He even went so far as to molest a little boy in the back seat of his parents' automobile while they were conversing with him from the front seat. The parents so trusted him, the child was so groomed and intimidated, that it was not discovered. He told the story with glee after he was caught much later. He told that story with pride, satanic pride.

Even after his heinous acts were discovered, the numbers of children violated unveiled, many people in the church did not believe it. After all, he was so "nice," and they would cite his helpful activities and mannerisms.

Does this remind you of Ted Bundy? Bundy eventually confessed to atrocities of which macabre nightmares are made. Yet, with horrific, irrefutable evidence compiled and with his stated confession, he still had friends saying, "This cannot be true. He is the nicest man I have ever met."

There is much to learn from this. First and foremost, we need the Holy Spirit. We need to be discerning. We cannot be naive or gullible. Jesus Himself did not commit Himself to all men because He knew them. We must learn this. (John 2:24)

God said, "Be wise as a serpent and innocent as a dove." Please, for children's sake, be "wise as a serpent" first. That is, pray to understand human behaviors. It is balance and power to know that the understanding of human behaviors must precede innocence. (Matthew 10:16)

This is not to say that all seemingly nice people are pedophiles. It is to say, we need to listen to children. We need to examine evidence when someone is accused. Do not dismiss "checks-nudges" in your spirit, or the voices of children, or compelling evidence, because people in any position in the church, or school, or family, etc. are "nice."

Please take a moment to read the "technique of the BIG LIE" taught by Hitler. It is accurate to say that the following issued forth from the father of lies, Satan, and then taught to his follow-er, Hitler. It is also a technique Satan continues to teach to his pedophiles. His point being to destroy generations of God's children.

(Please also remember that *Roe v. Wade* was another BIG LIE. Jane Roe, whose real name is Norma McCorvey exposed her lie first in an interview with World Net Daily. Wonderfully, Ms. McCorvey became a Christian in 1995.)

"The source of BIG LIE technique is this passage, taken from Chapter 10 of James Murphy's translation of *Mein Kampf*:

> *"But it remained for the Jews, with their unqualified ca-pacity for falsehood, and their fighting comrades, the Marxists, to impute responsibility for the downfall pre-cisely to the man who alone had shown a superhuman will and energy in his effort to prevent the catastrophe which he had foreseen and to save the nation from that hour of complete overthrow and shame. By placing responsibility for the loss of the world war on the shoulders of Luden-dorff they took away the weapon of moral right from the only adversary dangerous enough to be likely to succeed in bringing the betrayers of the Fatherland to justice. All this was inspired by the principle - which is quite true within itself - that in the BIG LIE there is always a certain*

force of credibility; because the broad masses of a nation are always more easily corrupted in the deeper strata of their emotional nature than consciously or voluntarily; and thus in the primitive simplicity of their minds they more readily fall victims to the BIG LIE than the small lie, since they themselves often tell small lies in little matters but would be ashamed to resort to large-scale falsehoods. It would never come into their heads to fabricate colossal untruths, and they would not believe that others could have the impudence to distort the truth so infamously. Even though the facts which prove this to be so may be brought clearly to their minds, they will still doubt and waver and will continue to think that there may be some other explanation. For the grossly impudent lie always leaves traces behind it, even after it has been nailed down, a fact which is known to all expert liars in this world and to all who conspire together in the art of lying."

- ADOLF HITLER, Mein Kampf

Sounds like Hitler made a pact with the father of lies, doesn't it? Let us remember that the "art of lying" is fathered by a defeated foe. Our God has overcome the wicked one. And we are to do the same.

Kindness vs "nice": Nice is a social skill and can be learned. Kindness is a spiritual fruit and is divinely developed by Christian character.

"What is desired in a man is kindness, And a poor man is better than a liar." - Proverbs 19:22

While "nice" can be a product of the "art of lying", it will not prevail against genuine kindness. Kindness is a fruit of the spirit and we are told no law can prevail against the fruit of the spirit. (Galatians 5:22-23) God will reveal to us the distinctive difference between the facade of "nice" and the genuine kindness of the spirit. (Matthew 7:16) We can trust Him in this matter as in all others. We can and should expect the "nice" liars to be exposed. Authentic, spiritual kindness, can and should be discerned by the people of God. We must learn to ask God, and then listen. We must pray that the "eyes of our understanding be enlightened." Ephesians 1:18

"Then Jesus said to those Jews who believed in Him, "If you abide in My word, you are my disciples indeed. And you shall know the truth, and the truth shall make you free."

- John 8: 31-32

Our God calls us to know the Truth, tell the Truth, discern the Truth, and teach the Truth. It is Truth that abiding in Christ unmasks and defeats lying. Let us therefore abide.

PRAYER: *Father, we praise You for the Holy Spirit of Truth. We are grateful for and covet Your wonderful gifts, specifically the Word of Wisdom, the Word of Knowledge, and the Discerning of Spirits. We praise You that we are partnered with You to win the war for our children. We praise You for Truth. We know that all lies and liars will bow to the King of Kings and the Lord of Lords. Forever, our Lord, Your Word is settled in Heaven and on earth. We commit Lord, to abide in Your Word and to be your disciples indeed. We praise you for the Word of Truth that has made us free. We teach and instruct our children how to abide in Truth and to be free. We do this with great joy. We believe in You and we love You. In Jesus Name. Amen.*

O is for OFFENSE

"Whosoever therefore shall humble himself as this little child, the same is the greatest in the kingdom of heaven. And whoso shall receive one such little child in my name receives me. But whoso shall offend one of these little ones which believe in me, it were better for him that a millstone were hanged about his neck, and that he were drowned in the depth of the sea. Woe unto the world because of offenses! for it must needs be that offenses come; but woe to that man by who the offense comes!"   - Matthew 18:4-7

In this teaching, Jesus demonstrates that the "greatest in the kingdom of heaven" are children. He teaches that not only are children Heaven's greatest, but also that adults are to convert and be "as" they are. How they are is innocent, and teachable. Children are born into this world ready to trust God. They are born belonging to God and are spiritually alive to God.

Jesus states that to receive a child is to receive Him. That is a weighty statement, significant and majestically meaningful. The word "receive" means among other things to "embrace," and "to receive into one's family." Clearly, rejecting a child is by Jesus' statement, a refusal of Him. He has placed Himself in the life of every child. The devil knows this and hates Him and His future ones. (Strong's Concordance)

Jesus said "woe to that man by who the offense comes!" To begin to understand this requires a definitional breakdown of the word "offense."

The word *offense* is "*skandalizo*" in the Greek language and is a strong word. The English word "scandal" is derived from it. This word and its shades of meanings cause clarity in just why the enemy is determined to target and molest children.

Each of the following definitions of this word sheds light on the demonic reasoning and demonic quest to violate God's children and thus attack Jesus.

Offense: *"to put a stumbling block or impediment in the way, upon which another may trip and fall, metaphorically to offend."* This is from the Greek Lexicon - Strong's 4624 and amplifies the definition in the following ways:

1. *"to entice to sin*
2. *to cause a person to begin to distrust and desert one whom he ought to trust and obey*
   a. *to cause to fall away*
   b. *to be offended in one, i.e. to see in another what I disapprove of and what hinders me from acknowledging his authority*
   c. *to cause one to judge unfavorably or unjustly*

3. *since one who stumbles or whose foot gets entangled feels annoyed*
   a. *to cause one displeasure at a thing*
   b. *to make indignant*
   c. *to be displeased, indignant"*

All of these definitions are seen in the results of child molestation. The enemy knows that sexual violation of innocence can produce all of these. To molest a child is to attack the spirit of life in that child. It is an attack that distorts and eliminates their willingness to "trust and obey".

One violated may spend years denying God or any other authority in their lives. The Living God, that a child is born willing and wanting to "trust and obey", often becomes The One from which they wish to hide. Sexual violation may cause major hindrances against all legitimate authority figures. Sexual violation causes a range of hindrances that produce "stumbling blocks." It causes "distrust" and often is used to cause a person to "desert" God, His plan, and a "normal" path of spiritual and emotional growth.

The greatest danger to the enemy's intentions is the heart, obedience, and salvation of God's children. When he is able to alter the greatness of a child by "offense," then that child's acceptance of Christ may be difficult and seriously thwarted. That "offense" also affects adversely the entire family, entire generations, and our future. (Please see "S is for Statistics.")

How offensive then is this "offense" to Christ? His own words, " ... *better that a millstone should be hanged about his neck and that he were drowned in the depth of the sea.*" A millstone signifies a weight that causes one to sink with no chance of surfacing. The offender is thrown into the depths of the sea, not a shallow part. There is no chance of escaping these circumstances. This statement by the Savior of the world deserves study and pondering. Remember, that Christ said, this would be the "better" thing for the offender.

"But whoso shall offend one of these little ones which believe in me, it were better for him that a millstone were hanged about his neck, and that he were drowned in the depth of the sea."
- Matthew 18:6

That sounds so terminal. That is so terminal. In our society many have learned to "pet and feed the offenders, the pedophile." Please don't.

It is never our desire to incite flesh anger or flesh action. It is our desire that every adult allow this teaching from our Savior to be a wake-up call. The very least this teaching should produce is awareness and a determination to protect children. Jesus made some strong statements. We are to take strong action.

We must become powerful for our children. We must pray and act to alter laws that by their ease, provide permission for offenders to continue their corrupt course.

Jesus is also teaching here a call to prayer. In verse 10, He states, *"That in Heaven their angels do always behold the face of My Father which is in Heaven."* We are instructed to seek His face and that His angels who excel in strength hear and respond to the Voice of His Word. Psalm 27: 8 and Psalms 103:20.

We are to pray the Word for the children of the nations and expect supernatural help. We are not limited to our own abilities to keep our children safe, but we are not to disregard our own responsibilities and abilities. There is a place where the practical and the supernatural meet. We are to do all that we can in the natural and God will meet us at that point with His supernatural power.

"What's done to children, they will do to society."
- Dr. Karl Menninger

I would add, what is done for children, they will do for God's Kingdom and that will affect society and establish His plan for all eternity.

PRAYER: *Father, we praise You and receive supernatural help for innocent children. Praise You for the ministry of angels. As we confess Your help and power, we do know that You are dispatching angels to guard over our children. We will teach our children the power of their own confession of Your Word. We thank You for the Anointing that makes us effective in our responsibility and equipped with abilities and heavenly help. Our prayer is that we activate and do all the good that we can and expect*

Your supernatural help as well. We do thank You for these little and great ones that have Your Heart. In Jesus Name. Amen.

P is for PORNOGRAPHY

"For the love of money is a root of all kinds of evil, for which some have strayed from the faith in their greediness, and pierced themselves through with many sorrows."   - 1 Timothy 6:10

The pornography industry in the natural realm is about money. The annual worldwide pornography profits are estimated to be well over $60 billion (yes, billion) dollars. It is not possible to estimate the numbers of people, God's creation, who are deceived and led by it. Realizing that there are over 7 billion people in the world may help put some perspective to it.

The Bible teaches a principle that applies to all humans. It is simply this:

> What we pay attention to we will desire.
> What we desire we will determine to attain.

This lesson has been learned well by the advertising media and they use it most effectively. That's why we are blitzed with product advertising. We see it, sometimes sing it, desire builds, and we buy. That is a principle of purchase.

Pornography in the natural realm and spirit realm works like a tsunami in that only one drop is not a reality. It accumulates and can become the master of the soul. And that is also why the world's system is determined to bombard us with it. It is a visual and destructive device that comes from the enemy of God. Pornography is the devil's "hot selling" product.

Pornography is a root of destruction that presents and produces pictures inside the soul that can eclipse all other vision. As an example of its power, the serial killer Ted Bundy, told how he started with the <u>Playboy Magazine </u>(yes, that is porn) and his flesh desire increased for more and for worse pictures. He is one of many molesters who have shared that pornography was the instrument providing their visions before their dark acts. Those pornographic images can rapidly block all other visions. In fact, it can so rule in the soul, that the dark pawns of Satan enter in and take control of the mind. The viewer then often becomes a vessel of demonic force acting out that demonically devised vision.

Ted Bundy terrorized the nation from 1974 until his capture in 1979. He was attractive, educated, and gifted in law and politics, extremely charming and "nice." He was also a brutal killer who raped and killed an untold number of women across the country. He committed atrocities that are too vile to record. Ted Bundy confessed to 30 murders, but authorities believe the true number of victims totaled over 100.

After 10 years on death row, Bundy was executed on January 24,1989. Shortly before his death, he was interviewed by Dr. James Dobson.

In Ted Bundy's conversation with Dr. Dobson, he stated, *"I've lived in prison for a long time now and I've met a lot of men who were motived to commit violence just like me. And without exception, every one of them was deeply involved in pornography."*

Bundy shares that pornography *"snatched him out of his home"* as a young child and that young people, *"walk past a magazine rack full of the very kinds of things that send young kids down the road to be Ted Bundy's."*

While one could reasonably doubt the veracity of Bundy, he was facing eternity and he seemed to want to share the root of his criminal acts while not denying his own responsibility.

Law Enforcement will also attest to the fact that pornographic material is almost always found in the homes of sex criminals.

One source of this fact is <u>Family Life</u> by Dennis and Barbara Rainey.

The full death row interview can be found on the following website: Pure Intimacy - Fatal Addiction: Ted Bundy's Final Interview <u>www.pureintimacy.org/f/fatal-addiction-ted-bundys-final</u> interview/

If you are "playing" with pornography in any form, please get help immediately. We are not saying that everyone will become a Ted Bundy, but we can absolutely say that you will become something you are not called to be, and that descending degrees of darkness will be your pathway. This is not a dramatic statement for effect, this is truth stated to alert and spare you, and those who love you.

Temptation: for those who may sense an urge to commit a sin against a child..."if your hand offend you, cut it off ... if your eye offend you, pluck it out". The hand represents an extension of a person's power of authority and the eye represents vision. If your thought life is reaching into these areas of dark vision, get help now. Do not think you can handle this matter alone. There are many good pastors and counselors whom God has already provided to help you.

One of the most devil-deliberate visions is child pornography. The viewing of child pornography is on an increase around our world.

<u>Thorn</u>, the Digital Defenders of Children list some alerting statistics:

"The National Center for Missing and Exploited Children (NCMEC) reviewed 22 million images and videos of suspected child sexual abuse imagery in its victim identification program in

2013 - more than a 5,000% (yes, 5,000%) increase from 2007.

19% of identified offenders in a survey had images of children younger than 3 years old; 39% younger than 6 years old; and 83% younger than 12 years old.

State and local law enforcement agencies involved in internet crimes against children task forces reported a 230% increase in the number of documented complaints of online enticement of children from 2004 to 2008." THORN

The devil is not just insidious with his tools of pornography; he is combustive. Do not forget that this is a "root" that produces ruinous "fruit". Ruin is always the result, always.

The very least pornography does is cause a person torment of the soul. The worst it does is cause a person to lose control of their own soul and to then to perform acts of torment on others.

It has been said and is true, that we cannot un-see things. Once viewed images can re-appear like flash cards in our soul. We win against them by mind renewal, but we will also have to fight for our mind's vision rights. We will have to strongly determine to take custody of our soul.

The Bible teaches that God's people perish for lack of vision. That is, vision of Him. The plot of evil is not only to steal God's vision of Him, but to insert his filth and propel us to filth action. Praise God, we can have victory in vision, of God and of ourselves. (Proverbs 29:18)

Even in the natural you cannot show two videos on a screen without causing distortion and confusion. It is greatly more confusing in the spiritual realm. That is one reason Job *"made a covenant with his eyes"*. (Job 31:1)

Our culture is saturated with sexual images. Our culture encourages children to present themselves in a provocative manner for monetary gain. Whether that is media advertising to sell items ranging from cereal to toothpaste, to present children as sexually suggestive fashion queens or kings, or the hard core porn industry, the result for children is victimization.

We are called to guard our hearts and minds from the visual bondage of so-called soft porn to hard core porn. We are called to personal protection and child protection.

Obviously our world is being flooded with pornography. Pornography is the root of destruction. The good news is our God is never without materials to build an "ark" of safety and victory.

One help toward keeping ourselves clean in this corrupt culture is the three second rule. It works like this ... the first second we see pornography in any form we register what we are seeing ... the next second we recognize the assault against our soul ... the third second we resist by turning away or turning it (television, Facebook, etc) off ... the fourth second the recording starts in our psyche. Yes, it is that fast and that simple. Simple as one, two, three. Do not wait for that fourth, recording second.

Children can learn the three second rule as well, and we should instruct them.

1. Register what we are seeing.
2. Recognize the assault against our soul.
3. Resist by turning away or turning it off.
   Resist the Recording of any pornography.

Yes, in a matter of seconds. In seconds, we can *"redeem the time"* because the days are evil. (Ephesians 5:16)

I heard the "Three Second Rule" years ago while involved in mental institution ministry. I wish I could give proper credit to the person who initiated it, but I have long since forgotten. It works and that is the essential credit.

This may indeed seem a small response for so large a dilemma. We must not despise small beginnings; we must simply begin. We must "do and teach" resistance to pornography in all it's dark form and demonic fashion.

"I have made a covenant with my eyes; Why then should I look upon a young woman?" - Job 31:1

"I dictated a covenant (an agreement) to my eyes; how then should I look (lustfully) upon a girl?" - Job 31:1 *(Amplified)*

"Submit yourselves therefore to God. Resist the devil, and he will flee from you." - James 4:7

It is wise to notice that submission to God is written first so that you will want to resist the devil. Remember, that Satan is a cunning enticer, who prompts you to "think" that you can handle a "drop or two" as he disguises the very real tsunami you are facing.

PRAYER: *Father, help us to see Your vision of life. Help us to teach and instruct others regarding the power of vision. Praise You that You instruct us and teach us in the way we should go; that You guide us with Your Eye. We mandate that our eyes be in covenant with Your Eyes so that we may act on Your Word. We praise You that we wrestle not against flesh and blood, but against principalities, powers, rulers of the darkness of this world, and spiritual wickedness in high places, and as we take authority in Your Name, we win this thing. Praise You that You inhabit the praises of Your people. In Jesus Name. Amen.*

Q is for Qualify

The pedophile and hebophile molesters often seek that child that "qualifies" to them as an opportunity to violate.

Qualify is defined as *"to describe or recognize someone, describe or portray the character of the qualities or peculiarities of, meet the requirements."*　　　　New Oxford American Dictionary

We use the term when describing what "qualifies" an "at risk" child.

An "at risk" child is defined with a variety of different indicators. Some of which are:

Child Traits
Limited reading proficiency
Prior abuse or trauma
Disability or illness
Behavior problems
Poor social skills
Poverty

Family Traits
Single parenthood
Welfare dependency
Family dysfunction
Abuse
Parental mental illness
Parental substance abuse
Family discord or illness
Not owning a home (an
　　often uprooted child may
　　exhibit insecurity)

This list, while accurate, is not all inclusive. However, for a caring parent, guardian, or pastor, these are definitely accurate alerts. Every child care worker in church or secular system should be aware of these conditions. Children that fit into these categories are vulnerable and could become victimized, prey for the predator.

It is negligent not to be aware and watchful. That may seem a strong statement, but the record proves that these "qualifiers" are far too often the door of opportunity for the stealthy sexual predator.

It is usual for a sex offender to watch for and identify these children in "at risk" conditions. Unfortunately for children, the offenders do educate themselves in child conditions. They have a watchful, educated in vulnerabilities eye, and will wait to pounce.

One predator joined a church and quietly waited (lurked) in the background of involvement for over eight months. In fact, he was so clever, and yes, "nice" that he had no need to seek working in children's church. The "nice", faithful in church attendance man was asked by church staff to help. It did not take him long to see which child was on the edge of the group and became his first, not even close to his last, victim.

One videoed interview with a youth minister, serial offender, while he is repulsive to the core, was helpful in the education of prevention. He shared how he simply ingratiated himself within the church, became "loving" and "helpful" to the Body, and waited months before molesting a child, an "at risk" child. Of course, no one believed the child and by then he had developed a staunch adult group of Christians who supported his "clean" character. Most of his little victims fit into the listed categories. Only a few did not. As stated, it is not an all inclusive list for victimization. Dark people like this "youth minister" like to branch out into the seeming healthy families as it stimulates their "game mentality".

One united statement regarding this committed pervert was, "he is such a nice young man." (See N is for Nice)

In his videoed interview he reveals how he delights in his game playing and skilled deceit. His statement was, "How easy it is to fool Christians." During the interview he dropped his "nice" persona and the real fiend appeared.

He did not permit the interview because he was remorseful or repentant. Not at all. He just took glee in displaying his ability to deceive. And he enjoyed the attention of the interviewer. Like his master, the devil, he considered those he deceived as fools, and those children he violated as inconsequential objects.

We are not to panic. We are to pray. We are to learn to "see" with God's Eyes. We must learn to respond to that "still, small, voice" and to respond to the Holy Spirit.

Again, and again, and always, children deserve and need our vigilance. Let us remember that God is our very present Help in trouble. "At risk" children may well be conditioned for trouble. But, there is a Mighty God, who when called upon is present and has prevailing power.

We are to recognize an "at risk" child so that we may release God's protective power in prayer. We are to recognize "at risk" children so that we may do all we can in the practical/natural to protect them as well.

Church staff should learn the definitions of "at-risk" children not just for a protective eye, but also to be vital instruments of God for the children. Offenders can be thwarted if they see that the staff includes all children in the activities. If the church staff is careful to hug all the children, disallow any sort of bullying, engage in conversation with all, draw peripheral ones into the group, they may well aid in disqualifying those children.

This of course, is the staff that has been background checked. Most Law Enforcement will also provide records of accusations or other offenses if they are asked. If there are any doubts or concerns about any one, at least ask. Having known someone for a long time is not a background check. It is a history and not an omniscient one at that.

We need to know all that we can about our children at home and at church. And please do be patient with, and love and guard the qualifying "at-risk" ones.

Under the leadership of the Holy Spirit we should also be seeking a love path into their homes and be a blessing in any way that is His way. Pray about it. When the answer comes, act on it. We must help these children.

PRAYER: *Father, we call upon You. We ask You to unmask the enemy and teach us to see. For Your children's sake and safety, we ask, believe, and receive, vision beyond and behind the appearance of man. We want, like You, to see the heart, the real motive and intent of people. Jesus, our Savior, did not commit Himself to all men, because He knew them. We ask, believe and receive this insight also. Praise You, Lord for the privilege of watching Your children. Help us to redefine "at risk" children as our "attendant responsibility" children. In Jesus Name. Amen.*

R is for REPENTANCE

While the subject of repentance for a child molester has been referenced in other "letters," it is a large subject and requires fuller understanding and questioning.

The question is, "Can a committed, habitual, addicted, demon motivated, child sex offender stop molesting, change, and become a successful human being?"

I have posed that question to those whose dominant field of work is with child sex offenders, members of the Federal Bureau of Investigation (FBI), Central Intelligence Agency (CIA), other Law Enforcement and the Instructors of such organizations. The answer from those who are experienced, studied, and deeply involved all have said the same, "I have never known one to change. The only way to trust one is if they say not to trust them around children". And, by the way, that last statement is rarely made by them.

There are several studies on recidivism. The following quotes are from the Office of Justice Programs, SMART- Office of Sex Offender Sentencing, Monitoring, Apprehending, Registering, and Tracking.

"Recidivism has been conceptually defined as the reversion to criminal behavior by an individual who was previously convicted of a criminal offense (Maltz, 2001). It reflects both the individual's recurrent failure to abide by society's laws and the failure of the criminal justice system to "correct" the individual's law-breaking behavior (Maltz, 2001). While the etiology of criminal behavior is complex (see chapter 2, "Etiology of Adult Sexual Offending," in the Adult section) and recidivism results from a range of personal and social factors, it is important to

recognize that recidivism is not simply another term for repeat offending. Rather, it refers to the recurrence of illegal behavior after an individual experiences legal consequences or correctional interventions imposed, at least in part, to eliminate that behavior or prevent it from occurring again (Henslin, 2008).1

"Perhaps the largest single study of sex offender recidivism conducted to date was carried out by Langan, Schmitt, and Durose (2003). The study, which was published by the U.S. Department of Justice, Bureau of Justice Statistics, examined the recidivism patterns of 9,691 male sex offenders released from prisons in 15 states in 1994. These offenders accounted for about two-thirds of all male sex offenders released from state prisons in the United States that year. Using a 3-year post-release follow-up period, rearrest and reconviction rates for sexual and other crimes were reported for the entire sample of sex offenders as well as for different categories of sex offenders." by Roger Przybylski (SMART)

It is important to know the definition of recidivism and to see the results of this largest study of it. We need to be alerted and informed. We must be wise.

This is sometimes a large dilemma for Christians. Over and over we hear of children being molested by those offenders who have declared repentance. There are individuals and groups of Christians all desiring to believe this "sin" is under the Blood as any other sin. They think it non-Christian not to give them another chance and trust them. They often cite the woman taken in adultery in John 8 or the David and Bathsheba story as well as "love covers a multitude of sins", etc. as their biblical position. These are real victories above sin; that's true.

But we need to see what Jesus said in proper application of scripture toward offending His children.

"But whoever causes one of these little ones who believe in Me to sin, it would be better for him if a millstone were hung around his neck, and he were downed in the depth of the sea."

- Matthew 18:6

The very least that should be derived from the declaration of Jesus is how very seriously He sees child offense. We should not gloss over this. There are children depending on us to understand God's Word and receive it appropriately.

There are strict guidelines to repentance. It is not a matter of what we want to believe about an individual; it is a matter of what is true regarding that individual. Repentance is not a work of human resolve or being sorry. True repentance is prompted by a Bible belief and a divine desire.

Flesh appetites, cravings, habits and resulting actions may be restrained by human resolve. But most people who have tried to quit cigarettes, drugs, alcohol, or other habits of strength, teach us that human resolve is often a weak tool that proves ineffectual. Most of us could even share the difficulties of flesh resistance to achieve healthy diets, fasting, exercise, or other things that are beneficial for us.

Now compound that with an accurate understanding of demonic compulsion combined with the decadent flesh lust that depicts a child molester. Factor in that it is documented ad nauseam that they say, "it is not their fault; they did nothing wrong," and that it is their glee to "fool all, especially Christians" and hopefully we can see why "repentance" from them has to be more than much of Christ's Body has required. It has to be beyond our naive or gullible false hope.

The word "repentance" is defined as *"a change of mind, as it appears to one who repents, of a purpose he has formed or of something he has done, to express sincere regret at what one has done"*. The operative word here is "sincere". (Greek dictionary, Strong's 3341)

Psalm 51 delivers a picture of repentance in 19 verses. David's sins were many, including adultery, conniving, murder, lies, betrayals and lack of trust in God. He repented, and, yet, there were still consequences.

David did not molest children. The requirements of true repentance listed however, could apply to a molester of children. It starts with:
- realization of sin
- ownership of responsibility for sin
- believing in God and asking for His mercy

Repentance continues with desiring cleansing from sin and knowing that the acts of sin were evil. Most molesters can only fake this so far, and we must remember they are skilled in phony affectation.

One known molester is a "repentant type". He attends church regularly, lifts his unholy hands, sings, and declares Christ. He exhibits all the signs of a wonderful Christian father, and, yes, he is very "nice." His present wife is also very "nice" and participates in molesting youth with him. When he was caught molesting and raping a young "at-risk" girl (he is a hebophile) he was very sorry. He knows what to say and how to say it. Due to some legal snares, he got away with serial molesting and rape. He has a background of molestation and rape of young "at risk" girls and boys. Some who know of his destruction of children, say, "he has changed." Others who do not know, say, "he is just too nice for it to be true."

Those of us in Law Enforcement and ministry positions know all too well that it is not only true, but also that there is nothing at all "nice" in this molester. I wish with all my heart that his was the only story like this. It isn't.

I do know that God has all eternity to catch up with him and his wife. In the interim, I do expose them when I hear they are attempting to become involved in a church. Could they repent? I only know they have not. Do they say they have? Yes, but they continue molesting.

We have so called ministers today who declare there is no need for repentance. They pervert the Gospel of Jesus Christ. They may sadly end up as a haven for fools and perverts. Repentance is always necessary. Repentance is real. Repentance can be lived out, and is only proven over a period of time.

Pastoring for many years we certainly have known that sex offenders attend church. We simply had them sign a contract which included an agreement of where and with whom they sat. There were restrictions on where they could be on the property. They were tagged for recognition by certain people on the Helps Team.

Some chose not to sign the contract and left. Some broke the contract and were asked firmly to leave and not return. We let other churches know who they were.

Some might say, "Why not give them a chance?" And I would answer, "A chance to do what?" Children must be our focus and priority. Why not give our children a chance?

Again, if there is sincere repentance they would avoid children like a sincere ex- alcoholic avoids bars and alcohol.

So, how do we know if repentance is genuine? Only time can declare a proven life. And I believe with all my being, that with a child molester, unless you hear, "you cannot trust me with children" and see their avoidance of children, it is not genuine. And even then, guard your child as they can learn to say any statement that furthers an evil intention.

Extreme to your thinking? Check the statistics. Re-read the SMART information on recidivism. Read the testimonies. Talk with Law Enforcement. Reread Jesus Words in Matthew. Protect your child.

"Therefore bear fruits worthy of repentance,"   - Matthew 3:8
Repentance bears fruit. Fruit takes time to develop. Fruit is to be examined.

PRAYER: *Father, all the evil in this world can sometimes seem overwhelming. But above all, through all, and for all, You are more than enough. Your grace is sufficient and where sin does abound, grace does much more. We pray and shout Your grace. We declare Your greatness and yield to and operate in Your power. Help us to see clearly the covenant truth of good and evil and to apply Your Word accordingly. What You hate, we hate. Your love for children lives in us and we commit to see, hear, and do, the truth that sets them free. Thank You for living in us, empowering us to care and to dare to do the right thing. We love You. We love Your children. In Jesus Name. Amen.*

S is for STATISTICS

Statistics are simply *"a practice or science of a collection and analysis of numerical data in large quantities, for the purpose of inferring proportions in a whole from those in a representative sample."* - New Oxford American Dictionary

Simply put, they are numbers that reflect a condition. Numbers that can "numb" us or numbers that should add up to compel us to action.

Sexual abuse is much more prevalent than we want to admit or think about. The following information is from "Protecting Your Child in an X-Rated World". It is a Focus On the Family book and I highly recommend it. It is a powerful enlightenment regarding the link between sex-crimes and pornography.

There are other statistics complied by other sources and while there is some fluctuation, the one constant is that the numbers are shocking and sad. I pray, however, that they indeed compel us to act.

1. "One in five men have experienced sexual abuse before they were 18.
2. One in three girls will have experienced sexual abuse by the time they are 18.
3. Statistics, those numbers, reveal that 93% of children and juveniles who are sexually abused know their perpetrator.
4. One in every four women between the ages of 14 to 21 will have been sexually assaulted.

The typical molester will abuse more than 360 victims over his lifetime. In fact, according to Dr. Gene Abel at Emory University, *"the typical molester will successfully abuse from 30 to 60 children before he is caught the first time."* Protecting Your Child in an X-Rated World

I would add to that statement by Dr. Abel, that the "he" molester is just as likely to be a "she" molester. And isn't it difficult to even connect the words, "typical" and "molester"?

These are the statistics based on the victims that have spoken and told of the abuse. Consider that there are more victims who have not told of their abuse and what they have had to live through. Again and again, I share, that there are ways to die without leaving the planet.

To consider these numbers as real people, mostly children, can almost be overwhelming. We can feel crushed in that consideration. Yet, we must.

Not to horrify us further, but to propel us, consider this. Think of three little girls you personally know or five little boys. Which of those children do not matter? Yes, it is hard to do. But it should cause courage that follows outrage, courage that comes forth from the Lion of the Tribe of Judah.

Frankly, believers and non-believers alike, we must fight for our children.

These are the statistics that openly reveal the demonic plot to stop the following of Jesus Christ. It is so easy to see. Too many of our little ones have become victims in the demonic war for our souls.

The statistic information following shows what the enemy knows and what many of us have been ignorant of or chosen to ignore.

Ages at which Americans say they accepted Christ and became a Christian.

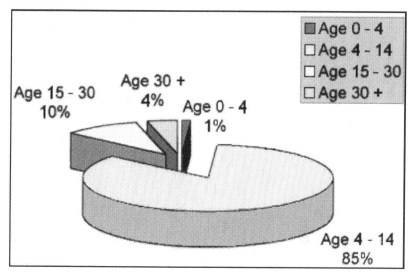

The data in the pie graph or chart comes from the Nazarene Church Growth Research.

Another survey -- by the International Bible Society -- indicated that 83% of all Christians make their commitment to Jesus between the ages of 4 and 14, that is, when they are children or early youth. The Barna Research Group surveys demonstrate that American children ages 5 to 13 have a 32% probability of accepting Christ, but youth or teens aged 14 to 18 have only a 4% probability of doing so. Adults age 19 and over have just a 6% probability of becoming Christians.

This data illustrates the importance of influencing children to consider making a decision to follow Christ.

Because the 4-14 period slice of the pie is so large, many have started referring to the "4-14 Window." Many people serving as career cross-cultural missionaries have testified that they first felt God calling them to missionary service during that 4-14 age period.

Please note the influence of the early Missionary Call that changes the world. Our children are innocents; they are also the hope and help of God's expansionism plan for the nations.

A statement often spoken regarding children is that they are "resilient." Resilient means *"able to recoil or spring back into shape after bending, stretching, or being compressed"* - *"able to withstand or recover quickly from difficult conditions."*

New Oxford American Dictionary

Speaking that "children are resilient" phrase, even if spoken often and sincerely will not make it true. Yes, they are "flexible" physically as they are growing and their bones are knitting together, but they do not "spring back into shape" after sexual molestation.

Sometimes it just takes time for them to absorb, assimilate, express, and display their brokenness. Our present world condition shouts that truth loudly.

"The world is a dangerous place, not because of those who do evil, but because of those who look on and do nothing."

Albert Einstein

PRAYER:
I am only one
But I am one
I cannot do everything
But I can do something
And by the Grace of God
What I can do and what I should do
I will do." In Jesus Name. Amen.

T is for TEN COMMANDMENTS

Commandments 1-5

Teach the Ten Commandments to your child with Authority, God's and yours. These Commandments were given by God to provide a sturdy and strong structure. As you share with your child you are building God's truth in them, and establishing a trust for God and for you.

During all the "Commandment Conversations", stop and listen for feedback. This is an excellent time to teach your child that you will always hear them simply by doing just that. They also learn that you set apart special times to listen to them. This special time, and you may even want to have a special listening place, is extremely comforting to a child.

Children are not automatic truth tellers. Sometimes they blurt out thoughts inappropriately and this has caused some to think them essentially honest. This is just not always the case.

It is during the "Commandment Conversations" that they can learn the high importance of truth telling. They will learn as they hear your high and exampled regard of honesty and the strength of your relationship and love. Your priorities will become their priorities.

"Foolishness is bound up in the heart of a child; The rod of correction will drive it far from him." - Proverbs 22:15

The word *foolishness* as defined by Strong's Dictionary can be defined as a *"fountain of foolish actions"*, and also describes the word as *"folly, or the power of fools, pre-eminence."* There is no doubt children like to feel important and often their "fountains" overflow with fantastical stories. They like to feel important, and they should be made to feel that way. We are to train and teach them the way of and importance of truth. They need to be trained.

There are many messages in the world and many media avenues of influence. For the protection of your child, get there first with God's message of power and protection.

An illustrated and simple understanding of the Ten Commandments will help us see the Father God's plan to protect and train children not just away from foolishness but into real faith.

Using our hands and fingers as illustration aids, we can teach our children the Ten Commandments and help shape their will and mind to place their trust in Him and us. That dual trust can greatly aid in prevention of our children being victimized by child molesters.

These are suggested dialogues. Please do adjust them for the best communication with your child.

The Ten Commandments empower us with loving laws of protection. The Ten Commandments could also well be described as Ten Connections of Relationships.

In the Bible, the 'Right Hand' denotes Authority. A reminder from "A is for Authority" is the definition of authority, which is defined as "the *power to give orders, make decisions, and enforce obedience*." (see Illustration 1.1)

1. There is only one God.

"We have only one God and Father, one God Who created us. He is above all, over all, and higher than all people and all things. He is a Covenant God and is our first and final authority. Covenant means that God has promised a relationship of commitment

with us. He makes and keeps promises because He loves us very much. We are to show our love to Him by keeping His command-ments. God is our loving and faithful Father. We have One God and He has three distinct personalities: God the Father, God the Son, and God, the Holy Spirit. They are One. That is sometimes hard to understand. It is just true. We are to believe that truth, even if we cannot fully explain it. We have only One God."

2. We are not to have or honor "graven images."

"Graven images" means anything that we might put our confi-dence in other than God. We are to worship only God. Nothing or no one deserves our worship and honor other than God. We place no image, or idol, such as statues or any person or thing over our honoring of God. We do not bow to any image. We bow only to God, who created us. God is not under anyone or anything. He is over all people and all things.

3. We do not take the Lord's Name in vain.

"Vain" means to use the Name of God or Jesus, or the Holy Spirit with a lack of respect. The Name of Jesus is powerful and to speak it without understanding or reverence, and respectful fear is like an ugly gesture. The Name of Jesus protects us and provides for us. Jesus Name opens a spiritual door and gives us supernatural help in times of trouble or fear. His Name is full of power. It is real power, not like the super heroes we sometimes see on television or in movies. His power is real. Jesus is real."

Note: Even very young children can be taught the protective provision available in the right use of That Name. Use the illus-tration to explain that some people use this finger as an ugly gesture. There are various ways to explain this depending on the age of the child. You may be mildly surprised at how even a very young child has comprehension of this.

4. We remember to keep God's Day His way, which means Holy.

"God has given us a day of the week to join together with others to worship Him and learn more about Him. This helps us grow stronger and makes us a better family."

"This finger of our hand is the weakest finger and helps us remember that we are weak, not as strong as God. Honoring a day of the week that He has set aside for us makes us stronger in His love, power, and authority. We have our immediate family and our church family. This week day is a time of rest from work and a time of refreshing for both families."

5. We Honor our parents in The Lord.

The smallest finger denotes parental authority. *"Our Father God is much bigger than I. However, He has placed me to be your parent. Because I recognize my place in your life, I am always seeking your safety and what is best for you as you grow. One reason I am your parent is to provide for and protect you. I want to be God's good parent to please Him and to bless you. I love you and will always want to listen to you. Under Father God, I am the first and final authority in your life. God has promised that as you honor your parents, He will give you a good and long life. That's what He and I want for you."*

Note: That small "finger" must be submitted to and be understanding of the commandments of one through four to be fully effective. Parents are positioned by God to help Him produce children with long and satisfying lives. This is the first commandment with promise, and is re-emphasized in Ephesians 6:1- 2. The destroyer, Satan, wants and seeks this place. His lust is to be the authority in your child's life and he motivates the predator-molester to achieve this dark goal. Your love of God, His plan for your child's long life, and your love for your child, must be protected. This truth cannot not be overemphasized.

"You shall teach them diligently to your children, and shall talk of them when you sit in your house, when you walk by the way, when you lie down, and when you rise up." - Deuteronomy 6: 7

PRAYER: *Abba Father, help us to teach the truth of Your Word as instructed in Deuteronomy 6: 7. We desire to equip our children in all these places and for all seasons and times. Help us, in our diligence to be both firm and fun. Let this time of instruction produce a fellowship with our children that strengthens them for every choice and decision in their life. I pray that Your Word hidden in their hearts, will keep them innocent and wise. Father, though parenting sometimes seems challenging, our faith is in You. We are filled with gratitude for the innocence of these children and honored to share Your Word for their lives. You have given us abilities and we will exercise them with Your counsel and help, as we prayerfully train these little people. We do recall how judgment came to Eli because he did not train his sons, and their own judgment as well. This causes us to see our great responsibility. It also causes great joy to know that you have invested in us Your Heart and plan for these valuable children. We praise You in and for this time with our children. Lord, we ask to see Your plan for each child and we will establish it their hearts and minds. We praise You for Your goodness and Your grace. We pray that our children serve You all their days and we will do our part to ensure that, with Your sufficiency. In Jesus Name. Amen.*

Right Hand
Illustration 1.1

The right thumb standing alone and over the other digits illustrate the first commandment. *There is only one God.*

The right indicator (pointer) finger shown as standing over and above the thumb illustrate the second commandment. *We shall have no gods before or over God.*

The right middle finger standing alone illustrates vulgarity and declares the third commandment.
We shall not take the Name of the Lord God in vain.

The right fourth finger is the weakest finger physiologically speaking and illustrates the fourth commandment of a Sabbath or week day for God.
Remember the Sabbath to keep it holy.

The smallest finger on the right hand illustrates the fifth commandment. *Honor your father and mother in the Lord.* It is smallest as parents are not equal God, but there is the authoritative responsibility to act with and for God.

The full right hand can be used to illustrate that all five fingers refer to the authority of God. If one were to slip on a red glove it would indicate that all five of these commandments fit into the one commandment in Matthew 22:37. *You shall love the Lord with all your heart, with all your soul, and with all your mind.*

Any color glove or mitten would do, but red would help illustrate the Blood Covenant of Christ.

U is for USING and UNDERSTANDING

Commandments 6-10

With the LEFT HAND we teach and illustrate how to love our neighbor and ourselves.

6. We do not murder.

"Sometimes people commit murder. A person limited in understanding, or who is led by darkness, or someone who thinks wrongly, is the person who commits murder. Murder means to take away someone's life. It is God who gives life and He does not want us to do that. Murder is a very wrong act.

Cain, in the Bible, murdered his brother, Abel. Cain did this because he was wrong in his actions toward God. Abel acted right and that made Cain angry. He thought on his anger so much it became all he could think about. Anger can turn to hate and that hate can make us very small people. Cain became a very small person and he murdered. He did not actually shrink in size; he reduced himself to small thinking.

God could not bless Cain, because he did an evil thing. While it is true that Abel went to Heaven with God, God did not want Cain to murder him. Cain made an evil choice."

Note: Murder includes abortion and suicide which usually are acts of selfishness or mental defect. This should be discussed according to the child's age, their questions, and their life experiences so far.

Killing for protection as in war, should be discussed with your child. It is good for a child to know that sometimes soldiers or police officers have to use force to protect us. Sometimes that means having to forcibly stop someone who would harm us. The distinction between the small mindedness of murder, and killing to protect should be discussed.

You might say, *"When a police officer or a soldier has to use force, it is to protect innocent people and to protect the freedoms that God wants us to enjoy."*

This is a good place to share your desire to protect your child. *"We want to protect you. We never want bad things to happen to you."*

Given the climate of the culture in which we live the distinction between murder and killing should not be disregarded.

7. We do not commit adultery.

"This is easy to remember as this is the wedding ring finger. On this finger we place a circle of covenant, a ring as a symbol of commitment. It is to serve as a reminder of God's love for us and His design and plan for marriage. It is a promise first to God and then to our marriage partner. When we marry we make a promise to honor all aspects of ourselves to our marriage partner. Sometimes when this promise is broken, it is broken with adultery. That means, what belongs to our marriage partner is given to someone else."

Note: This is a place for children of divorced parents to be told that the divorce was not their fault. Yes, they do all think that and at almost every age that the divorce takes place. There is an enemy who torments children with that false information: *"If I were a more obedient child, more lovable, hadn't said or done that ..."* etc. We need to stop the enemy by disallowing false information. The enemy's refrain can cause fear, insecurity and unworthy thinking. It is not the fault of the child. This information can heal the child and halt the plan of the enemy to further wound his or her soul. Please, tell them.

A young child who is not taught that his parents' failure in keeping that vow is not the fault of the child may become an "at-risk" child. It helps heal the hurt a child experiences to be told that they are guiltless and still very loved. They must be told that they are not the cause of parental failure. Parents can and should impart this truth without assigning blame to the other parent.

We wish it did not have to be said, but it does. Unless the divorced and other parent is the child's sex offender, please do not malign them to the child. It may feel good to you for the moment, but you risk hindering his or her identity and make them not only insecure, but a possible victim for the predator who seeks such damaged children.

This is also the place to share with children whose parents were not ever married, that God loves them and that they were formed and planned by Him before the foundation of the world. Build security in the child in every case. Assure them of your unchangeable love and that you are already praying for them, if it is the plan of God for them to marry, that they to do it once and well someday. The amount of the non-marital status information is again, contingent on the age and comprehension level of the child.

Information in "doses" is typically the best course. Usually a child will ask what they are questioning if the parent is calm and openly expressing love.

If your child was molested by a biological parent or stepparent, please seek Godly counsel if you have not yet done so.

Depending on the child's age, this is where we share God created two genders, male and female. It is His divine plan for a man to marry a woman. So many of our young children are bombarded with a homosexual agenda. This has become extreme in our culture and can cause great confusion in your child unless you share God's truth first and firmly.

Some states and schools are establishing an opening for the homosexual agenda. Some are even going as far as having small children kiss same sex friends for "understanding". So, please, do not be ignorant of the enemy's attempt to recruit children into this persuasion.

Note: The spirit behind the homosexual agenda is persuasive. They cannot procreate, so they (the spirits) must recruit to populate. In America, today, the homosexual persuasion path is in fast motion. Be there first, with God's truth for your child.

Remember, many sex offenders, while not homosexual, will molest boys or girls. It is not about gender preference, it is about child molestation.

Reiterate that God is good, and that marriage between a man and a woman is good. God said so, and He is Truth. Again, if you are speaking from a marriage failure position, it is imperative that your build security into your child.

8. We Do Not Steal

"Usually this is the longest finger and helps teach that we do not reach or extend into things that do not belong to us. Our God is good; He knows what we want and what we need. He will provide things for us. Sometimes we do not have things because we need to grow and be prepared to enjoy and to take care of them."

Share that like God: *"We, as your parents, want good things for you as well. Like God, we sometimes wait because you are not old enough or it is not good for you. Sometimes we adults do not have the means to get things right now. We are never too old to learn to wait on the goodness of God. We want to be sure that the things we have and how we get them, glorify our God."*

This is the place to share that you do not want your relationship with your child stolen, that no person is to be more important in your child's life than God and then you. Remind them that God has made you a family. Share that you take your family relationship very seriously and that you want your child to do so as well.

Suggestion to share: *"No one should ask you to keep secrets from us. The only time you are to keep information from us is when we are planning for holidays where we give presents and those presents are to be a surprise."*

Children should be taught the difference between secrets and confidentiality. *"Confidential means we may hide things for a short while as it will be a happy surprise when told. Secrets usually mean not to tell your parents something and maybe for always. Secrets are information hidden from your parents that can often make you feel uncomfortable or unsafe."*

"Secrets that hide things from mommy and daddy are not good. Do you have any secrets now?" is a good question. Be lovingly responsive to your child whether their answer is silly, sobering, or staggering.

9. Do not be a false witness. We do not lie.

(the pointing finger can be used to illustrate this truth. This is obviously a major place to build a trust relationship with your child.)

"We do not "point" at any one with false or untrue information. You may and should always tell me the truth about any fear or concern you may have. I will always listen and want to believe you. That is just one reason to tell the truth, so that you and I can always share openly and honestly. Of course, God, our Heavenly Father wants us to tell the truth."

Based on your child's age, this is a place to ask if they want/need to share/confess any untruths that may be between you. Then listen, really listen. Display your concern, your caring and tell them that nothing, absolutely nothing, will ever stop you from loving them, that just like our God, your love is unconditional.

Again, age contingent, you may wish to illustrate that lies are like a fabled dragon that stands between you and your child, and that if lies are not dealt with by truth, that fabled dragon treats it like food and it can grow bigger and bigger. Emphasize that you do not want anything between you hindering your relationship. Sometimes this jells overnight or even a few days as the child may wait and ponder your words. Children want to rely on your continued love and acceptance. When they feel confident of their safety, they will share.

Always train your face and tone to show love and understanding to the child no matter what they may share. Patiently wait for them to share it all as they will indeed be gauging your reaction as they unfold their situations. They may express their sharing in pieces of information and watch you as they reveal that information. They may share small disclosures, i.e. *"remember when you said do not take a cookie?, well, I did."* Be wise in your response, as the next revelation, whenever and whatever that may be, will depend on your reaction to the first one.

Do not prompt your child. This may lead to them affirming information that they think you want. Children are prone to pleasing.

If they think they are accomplishing this by agreeing with your promptings, they may do so. The last thing we want is to implant a fabrication in our children. If you have a hunch or suspicion, do not ask leading questions that can inadvertently plant a lie.

Illustration of implanting: *"Has cousin Bo touched you? Do you feel unsafe with cousin Bo"*, etc. This sort of questioning can be confusing to the child. It can help produce a non-truth to please the questioner. Again, most children tend toward people pleasing.

One of the most difficult facts to deal with is that children are so very often not believed when they do report sexual violation or physical abuse. We must teach them the power of truth and then trust them.

10. *We do not covet.*

"That means we do not want things that belong to other people or become envious of what others may have that we do not. Covet means we have a jealous feeling and want things that are not ours.

Sometimes, when we feel jealous, we need to remind ourselves that God loves us and gives us good things. We need to be patient for some things and trust God. He is our Provider. God is our Provider always.

Sometimes we need to wait for things because we are not mature or wise enough to use them yet. God wants me to provide for you as you grow. As your parent, I am the authority over your readiness to receive some things. I also am the person of authority over who gives you things as well. I have even asked Grandfather and Grandmother to check with me before they give you gifts. I love you so much and want you to learn to take care of things as well as receive them at the appropriate times. This is called stewardship and readiness. God blesses us amazingly as we learn stewardship and grow into readiness."

The (pinkie) finger on the left hand illustrates that people who do not have the largeness of the mind of Christ, who are then small minded, murder. This small finger illustrates the sixth commandment. *You shall not murder.*

The marital ring-bearing seventh finger illustrates the seventh commandment. *You shall not commit adultery.*

The middle and usually the longest finger on the left hand illustrates the eighth commandment by exampling a reaching beyond what belongs to us. *You shall not steal.*

The index finger on the left hand illustrates the ninth commandment by pointing at or accusing a person falsely. *You shall not bear false witness.*

The thumb on the left hand illustrates the tenth commandment. Because we have a covenant God we do not have to covet or long for things that do not belong to us. Our God provides. *You shall not covet.*

The full left hand can be used to illustrate the love God has poured into our hearts for others and for ourselves. A red glove placed on the left hand shows the fulfillment of Matthew 22:39. *You shall love your neighbor as yourself.*

Please note: One dark strength of a child molester is to identify the wants of your child and then stealthily or cloyingly provide them.

You may wish to complete the teaching by utilizing Matthew 22: 7-9. *"Jesus said unto him, You shall love the Lord your God with all your heart, and with all your soul, and with all your mind."* Illustrate this commandment by slipping your right hand in a glove. All five of the first Old Testament Commandments are defined and fit into the one New Testament Commandment written in Matthew 22:7.

"And the second is like it, You shall love your neighbor as yourself." The fullness of this truth, Matthew 22:8 is illustrated by slipping your left hand into a glove.

Children learn from this and with repetition, which they love, they can also learn to teach it, and they should.

Remember: Teach the Ten Commandments to your child with Authority, God's and yours. These Commandments were given by God to provide a sturdy and strong structure. As you share with your child you are building truth in your child and a trust in God and in you. His truth is the shield and defense for our children.

Start at an early age. Get the truth and trust of God's Word into your child. If "early" is too late, start now. Now is always a good time. Just get the Word sown.

"And you, fathers, do not provoke your children to wrath, but bring them up in the training and admonition of the Lord." Ephesians 6:4. Strong's Concordance defines "fathers" as either parent, or an older person.

PRAYER: *Father, we ask Your guidance in bringing these children up in the way they should live so that when they are old they will not depart from it. Help us to teach them to love You with all their spirit, soul, and body. Give us wisdom to teach them without frustrating them. Help us to be easily understood. We desire that these teaching and fellowship times be a joy for our children. Our heart's desire and prayer is that they love You and serve You everyday, that they have a holy and healthy self-awareness and still be other people centered. Abba Father, we praise You for every moment with our children. We are eager and enthusiastic teachers of little vessels of honor to You. We praise You. We desire that they walk worthy of You, fully pleasing You, and being fruitful in every good work and that they increase daily in the knowledge of You. In Jesus Name. Amen.*

V is for VICTORY

"For whatever is born of God overcomes the world. And this is the victory that has overcome the world - our faith." - I John 5:4

A major point of victorious understanding for believers is that we must not shun facts. We are required to look them squarely in the face and know that our faith in God overcomes or swallows facts. To ignore or fear them, however, is to give place to the enemy.

To see or to state a fact should not disturb or shatter our faith. Our faith should simply and powerfully see the victory that has been given us. Our faith in God diminishes and removes the power of negative or fearful facts. Facts should actually help activate our faith.

One great example that depicts the operation of facts and faith is shown in Numbers 13.

"Then Moses sent them to spy out the land of Canaan, and said to them, 'Go up this way into the South, and go up to the mountains, and see what the land is like: whether the people who dwell in it are strong or weak, few or many; whether the land they dwell in is good or bad; whether the cities they inhabit are like camps or strongholds; whether the land is rich or poor; and whether there are forests there or not. Be of good courage. And bring some of the fruit of the land.' Now the time was the season of the first ripe grapes." - Numbers 13: 7-10

Moses sent 10 spies out to garner facts. And he requested a full view and report of those facts.

He received back two different views:

View 1 depicts people who allow facts to overwhelm their faith.

"Then they told him, and said: 'We went to the land where you sent us. It truly flows with milk and honey, and this is its fruit. Nevertheless the people who dwell in the land are strong; the cities are fortified and very large; moreover we saw the descendants of Anak there. The Amalekites dwell in the land of the South; the Hittites, the Jebusites, and the Amorites dwell in the mountains; and the Canaanites dwell by the sea and along the banks of the Jordan.'"
- Numbers 13:27

"But the men who had gone up with him said, 'We are not able to go up against the people, for they are stronger than we.'"
- Numbers 13:31

The evil report they gave was not in the stating of facts. It was in their view of the strength of those facts. They declared in essence, *"Yes, God's fruitful promise is evident. But, the facts of the enemy are much greater than God."* That is the definition of an evil report.

View 2 depicts the people who recognize that while facts are to be considered, they are not bigger than God. Facts, regardless of size, numbers, or seeming ferocity, are not able to stop people of faith from achieving and fulfilling what He has promised.

"Then Caleb quieted the people before Moses, and said, 'Let us go up at once and take possession, for we are well able to overcome it.'"
- Numbers 13:30

Caleb did not dismiss the facts. He simply understood that God is bigger than any circumstantial facts.

The huge point is this: We are required by God to assess circumstances and situations. We are to recognize that there are enemies, lots of enemies, in all the places that God has given us while we occupy this planet called earth. We are not to allow those facts to overcome us. We, instead, are to overcome them.

In understanding the fight of faith against the evil assignments that would harm our children, we must be practical and spiritual. We cannot ignore facts. We are not supposed to ignore them, or be deterred by them, no matter how seemingly large and daunting they may appear. God has given us promises of protection, and we are to act on them, without being ignorant or afraid of facts.

In sharing the facts of child molestation with some, I have often felt like broccoli in their ice cream world. There are those who think that because they believe in God that all their "hunkies" are just automatically "dories". That is just not the case. We live in a world infested with facts of darkness.

Jesus said, in this type of world, we are to "be of good cheer, because He has overcome the world." And He has given us His tools to imitate Him and follow in His discerning and powerful steps. (John 16:33)

Yes, there are molesting "giants" in the land. But they are not bigger than our God and His Covenant. We can and must stand secure in the Might and Majesty of God.

Simply put, check out all the facts and believe to overcome. Swallow facts with faith and you will eat the good fruit of victory in every place and in every season.

Psalm 91 is the good and protective Word of God. It is not religious nor vain to speak it over your family daily. And it is wise to have your children learn it and meditate it as well. We desire and deserve, because of His Blood, to have "long and satisfying lives". God desires to "show us His salvation" in this land.

Today's battle, the war against children is also the Lord's. And He has given us His weapons: The Blood, The Name (Jesus), The Word, and His Praise. They are not carnal (flesh tools) but they are mighty. We speak and confess them in prayer. They affect and change the spirit realm and they pave the way of action in the natural realm.

CONFESSION (prayer): *"Father, thank You for giving us Your armor. Our loins are girt with truth and it is Your truth that makes us Your disciples and makes us free. We have on the breastplate of righteousness, that is we have the ability to stand in Your presence without any sense of guilt or feeling or inferiority. Our feet are shod with the preparation of the gospel of peace and as much as it depends on us, we live at peace with all men. We have on the helmet of salvation, so we are not conformed to this world, but we are transformed by the renewing of our minds. We have the sword of the spirit which is Your Word, and we know that You sent Your Word and healed us and delivered us from all destruction. We have the shield of faith and we are equipped to quench all the fiery darts from any level of wickedness. We are praying always with all prayer and supplication for all and especially for our children."*

PRAYER: *Father, we rejoice that we are equipped with Your armor and we stand together for a good report as we believe in You and Your Covenant Truth. We are well able to protect our children as You have so powerfully provided for us. Father, with Your Gifts and Your Fruit of Character, we are more than equipped to overcome the "giants" that would seduce and diminish our children and we praise You for it. We rejoice that as we speak Psalm 91, You then watch over Your Word to perform it. In Jesus Name, we have the victory. Amen.*

W is for God's WILL

"Even so it is not the will of your Father which is in Heaven, that one of these little ones should perish."   - Matthew 18:14

The word "perish" is defined as:
"to put out of the way entirely - abolish - put an end to - to ruin - render useless - to kill - to declare that one must put to death - to destroy". (Strong's Concordance)

It is easy to see the will of the devil in that one word definition. God does not want the enemy's will imposed on his "little ones."

God's Will is defined throughout all scripture. His Will and His Word are synonymous. In this one scripture, we can see a breakdown of His Will for all and especially His children:

"For we are His, workmanship created in Christ Jesus unto good works which God has before ordained that we should walk in them."   - Ephesians 2:10

These six points of understanding lead to His truth:

For we are His	... Whose we are
Workmanship created	... What we are
In Christ Jesus	... Where we are
Unto good works	... Why we are
Which God has before ordained	... When we are
That we should walk in them	... Walk of Christian conduct

That one verse answers 6 questions regarding God's Will and purpose for our lives. Children are birthed to live out these "W's." Adults are called to teach them.

The fallen angel, now Satan is determined to work his will against God's in all things and especially in the lives of "little ones." The following story is true and extremely difficult to read. Difficult to fathom that this could actually happen. But it does.

"Horrific details are emerging in a case out of Michigan where a man arraigned on 12 counts of first degree sexual misconduct admitted he sexually assaulted his 3-year-old daughter, "too many times to remember". The 27-year-old has also been accused of taking elicit photographs of her for his own sexual gratification and even made her watch child porn. His wife admitted she helped her husband penetrate their daughter by holding her hands, "so it wouldn't hurt so much" while he held her legs if she tried to get away.

The girl's mother who has a history of being sexually abused also admitted she and her husband watched pornography and had sex in front of the girl. She also said her husband has raped her too, and once grabbed her throat after she saw him physically abuse her sons when they were ages 2 and 4. He threatened to throw her out a window if she ever called the police.

Police got involved after someone called to report the girl's sexualized behavior, behavior that included "humping her stuffed animals" and asking her brother for sex. The details of the case were revealed in a petition filed by the Department of Human Services. They are seeking to terminate the man and wife's parental rights to their children.

The girl and two boys, now age 5 and 8, have been removed from the custody of the girl's mother and have been placed in foster care. The family had been living at the Avalon Hotel. The father says he is a sex addict with a gambling problem and has written an apology letter to his daughter that read, in part:

"If you're reading this, I am either dead or in jail. I am not proud of being here. I also was touched as a child and repressed its memory as long as I could. When we moved, that nightmare came back and haunted me and I unfairly took it out on you. I am sorry for what I have done and hope that you have a happy life wherever you end up. I know you are going to have a lot of questions as to why this happened and I can tell you that at this time, I am not fully sure as to why this happened. Please know that I want the best for you and I am going to get the help I need. My head is not right and hasn't been for a long time. I know that I can never take back what I did and can say sorry a million times."

*Michigan Live with Danielle Salisbury
in partnership with The Washington Post.*

Before too much sympathy is invested in the pedophiles letter of "remorse", you may wish to re-read it and count the times he references himself as opposed to the child. It is also worth noting that his quest for help is for himself. Pedophiles are typically slick at declaring remorse and turning it into a ploy that makes them the unfortunate victim. They typically attempt to minimize the evil they have done; as in, "I unfairly took it out on you." If you are unsure, then read it again, slowly. Is this adult couple beyond help? We do not know. We do know that there are at least three children who, with prayer and covenant help, may be able to realize the "W's" reality.

Re-read God's Will as defined in Ephesians 2:10. Do you see how the enemy of God's "little ones" has managed to *"kill, steal, and destroy"* the Whose, What, Where, Why, When and the Walk of three children?

Our quest is to focus on the children. They must be our priority no matter what else one may believe. I pray for these three children. We pray for all the children that the enemy thinks to have shattered. We pray that you will do so as well. We must become active so that God, our God, can produce for these children His beauty out of dark determination to cause ashes.

We live in a time where the enemy uses diffusion like a smoking opium pipe to blur our focus and thus the power of unified purpose. We must make His children, His greatest, our greatest concern.

Now is a good time to meditate on this encouraging truth, *"I had fainted unless I had believed to see the goodness of the Lord in the land of the living."* (Psalm 27:13)

Remember, as long as we are on this planet, God's goodness and His power are available to us. Let us believe for and act on that great prevailing truth.

"Silence in the face of evil is itself evil: God will not hold us guiltless. Not to speak is to speak. Not to act is to act."
Dietrich Bonhoeffer

Be encouraged in the prevailing power of God. He is not limited. God is intimately involved with us in the care of His "little ones". We have heavenly, supernatural help on this planet. God gives us sense, both common and covenant. He is in this season with us and we are to "Win This Thing". We are partners with Almighty God in protection of children.

"The test of the morality of a society is what it does for its children." Dietrich Bonhoeffer

To this I say, "Amen" and let us please, In Jesus Name, pass this test.

PRAYER: *Father, we call upon You, for You will hear us, O God; Incline Your ear to us, and hear our speech. Show Your marvelous lovingkindness by Your right hand, O You who save those children who trust in You from those the enemy uses to rise up against them. Keep them Lord, as the apple of Your eye. Hide them under the shadow of Your wings, from the wicked who would oppress them, and from the deadly enemy who desires to surround them. Lord, we praise You that You also heal those little broken hearted ones and surround them with songs of deliverance. Teach us to pray more effectively daily as we win this battle for Your children. In Jesus Name. Amen.*

X is for SEXUALIZATION

We need to be aware that sexualization is not cute, not at all. When an innocent child, boy or girl, is thrust into sexually mature situations, dressed and postured to produce a sexually mature image, confusion results. That state of confusion, orchestrated by the devil is devised to make that child a target. The enemy often uses this inappropriate "maturity" to entice the eye of the predator.

Should you subject your child to adult like attire, programs, or pageants, etc? Usually parents share that they use these adult like events as opportunities to promote their child's poise and confidence. The increasing concern with that thinking is the amount of worldliness that has seeped into these events. We may not be recognizing who is the real "promoter" of these competitions; and often, who is the loser.

We should ask ourselves these questions:

How old is my child and how old does this event make him or her seem?

How mature looking and acting is the group they are companioning with in this activity?

Is my child being viewed or judged by an outward appearance that would depict a more mature individual?

These are not trivial questions. All events in which we place our children should be carefully and prayerfully pondered. Perhaps we should seek opportunities that help gain and strengthen our children's confidence without producing contrived maturity.

The hope and goal is that all children are allowed to be children, innocent children. We are called to *"train them up in the way they should go"* (Proverbs 22:6), not inadvertently catapult them into pseudo adulthood and possible consequences that result from that. We must guard against causing conflict of identity in their souls.

Obviously, this is a parental decision. We simply strongly suggest that parents be armed with accurate information so that divinely developing childhood be our first and prioritized consideration.

Please also know that some sex-offenders excuse themselves from reality by stating that the child who appears mature, is mature.

And by the way, cussing/cursing is not "adult" language. It is a diminishing of the soul and seeds unrighteous fruit in the spirit realm that manifests in the natural realm. Curse words produce a dark place for an adult or a child. It is not cute when a child acts, cusses or behaves in ways that are typically and falsely known or thought of as "adult" mannerisms.

"Death and life are in the power of the tongue, and those who love it will eat its fruit."   - Proverbs 18:21

We certainly know that Wikipedia is not the Bible or the only source of information. However, the below description of the results of sexualization is accurate and supported by those who study and detail such data.

> *Wikipedia:*
> *"Sexualization (or sexualisation) is to make something sexual in character or quality, or to become aware of sexuality, especially in relation to men and women. Sexualization is linked to sexual objectification. According to the American Psychological Association, sexualiza-*

tion occurs when "individuals are regarded as sex objects and evaluated in terms of their physical characteristics and sexiness." "In study after study, findings have indicated that women more often than men are portrayed in a sexual manner (e.g., dressed in revealing clothing, with bodily postures or facial expressions that imply sexual readiness) and are objectified (e.g., used as a decorative object, or as body parts rather than a whole person). In addition, a narrow (and unrealistic) standard of physical beauty is heavily emphasized. These are the models of femininity presented for young girls to study and emulate." According to the Media Education Foundation, the sexualization of girls in media, and the ways women are portrayed in the dominant culture, is detrimental to the development of young girls as they are developing their identities and understanding themselves as sexual beings.

The sexualization of girls not only reflects but also contributes to sexist attitudes, a societal tolerance of sexual violence, and the exploitation of girls and women. Reports have found that sexualization of younger children are becoming increasingly more common in advertisements. Research has linked The Sexualization of young girls to many negative consequences not only for girls but society as a whole. Studies have made connections between sexualization and the impaired cognitive performance in college-aged women, and the viewing of sexually objectifying material can contribute to body dissatisfaction, eating disorders, low self-esteem, depression and depressive affect.

Sexualization of girls occurs almost everywhere in today's dominant culture, from media and advertisements, to clothing and toys marketed for young girls. In virtually

every source of media, including television, music videos, music lyrics, movies, magazines, sports media, video games, the Internet, and advertising, the sexualization of women and girls can be easily found."
Wikipedia, the free encyclopedia

Be encouraged to read that again. Your child is worth it. And so are you.

"Every child you encounter is a divine appointment."
Wess Stafford, President, Compassion International
"Too Small to Ignore: Why the Least of These Matters Most"

PRAYER: *Father, we know that Your Word teaches us to abstain from all appearance of evil. We believe also that Your desire is that we not inadvertently train Your children to appear as bait for evil eyes. Help us to achieve balance as we endeavor to lead and teach our children toward covenant maturity, confidence, and poise. We believe childhood to be that time where You orchestrate the unfolding personality of each child to achieve Your unique and holy plan. We praise You for eyes to see and ears to hear in the divine development of the wonderful little people You have entrusted to us. Thank You, Living God. In Jesus Name. Amen.*

Y is for YOUR PURPOSE

"The thief does not come except to steal, and to kill, and to destroy. I have come that they may have life, and that they may have it more abundantly."   - John 10:10

John 10:10 is a contest scripture. We see that Jesus came because He desires to give us His Life and abundant way of living. The "thief" that is the devil, has a threefold objective. He determines to "steal, kill, and destroy" God's life in us.

Let us unfold the enemy strategy for clarity and trustingly to prevent his corruption:

- he manipulates to *"steal"* our identity.
- he then *"kills"* by altering our passion.
- he then is positioned to *"destroy"* our purpose.

In this section we will look at his plot for destroying our purpose. Please read "I is for Identity" and "Z is for Zealous " for amplification of "steal and kill".

It is this simple: if the enemy can "steal" our identity, he can "kill" our passion and then "destroy" our purpose. Every person is created by God and He has a plan in His Mind for each one. The enemy's ultimate quest is to destroy our God-given purpose.

All babies are born with God's seed of purpose in them. Part of training up a child is to pray and also watch that child to discover his or her "seed-gift", and nurture it.

God has ordained adults with "seed-gifts" as well. We are called and gifted for vocations. Whatever that vocation may be, it is for our joy, satisfaction, and to glorify God. Our vocations should provide our finances and a sense of satisfaction. Doing our tasks well is job satisfaction.

He has equally ordained us with a gifting and common purpose for children. Jesus says in Matthew 18:5, *"Whoever receives one little child like this in My name receives Me."* He is teaching His disciples the definition of greatness as He draws a child into their midst.

The word "receive" in this verse as defined by Strong's Concordance means *"to receive into one's family, to bring up or educate."* It also means to *"receive favorably, give ear to embrace, make one's own, approve, not to reject."*

This verse in context could easily read, *"Disciples, do you want to be great? Do you want to receive and embrace Me? Do you want favor? Then all of you disciples/learners, must place children in your midst, and teach them and listen to them. Do not reject them for they are your family. Educate My children."* Jesus instruction in this verse is so large. We must study and apply this written truth.

All people are called to the guardians and teachers of children. It is a high and holy call. I think it to be a vital call to God's churches today. We must prioritize teaching, protecting, and listening to children.

We have shared the how and why of the enemy's determination to destroy the purpose of a child. He has been busy as well destroying the understanding of parental/adult purpose, He does it by:

Stealing the identity of parenting priorities and authority. The world system and media have made major strides in eroding the truth of parenting and God's placement of parental/adult power.

Killing parental passion. This is done with the increase of diffusion through broken homes, financial overloading, guilt, fear, anger, a sense of inferiority against the pseudo education and power of the world's system, a wearing down from lack of time, and on it goes. These all can cause a sense of helplessness that sometimes results in indifferent or passionless parenting. The world system works hard against parental position and power.

Destruction of a parent's purpose and power usually leads to the loss of the power and purpose of God in the child's instruction. God's Message, if stopped in the adult generation, ensures the loss of God's High Life for the parent now and the child now and in their future. (John 10:10)

That can sound dire and discouraging, a giving up place. But in every place, in every circumstance and situation, God will make a way where there is no way. He can and has provided a *"table in the wilderness"*. A table that is our provision for all our needs. (Psalm 78:19)

Parents often say they do not have the time to instruct, train, and maybe especially listen to their child. When we determine to teach God's children His way, He can and will lengthen the productive time in our days. (Proverbs 3:2) That is His Truth and we can count on it, absolutely. And how much more if we are determined to walk His way with His children. He has also given us help in the extended family and in His church.

Please note that the places of God's provision are His Family, His Body, and His Church. We must study and gain the truth delivered to us in Matthew 18. It was given to us by God and for His "little ones." This is a day for instruction and training in safety for children. We must "approve them, make them our own, and not reject them."

The following is a victory story. It is a message of protection for a child and the stopping of a predator from a successful abduction.

"Police in Houston, MO, are searching for a woman who tried to abduct a child from a Texas County business. It happened Tuesday around 2 p.m. on Highway 17.

Houston Police Chief Jim McNeill says a white female walked into the business and grabbed a 6-year-old girl by the arm. The child fell to the floor and began screaming.

The girl's mother started yelling when she heard the commotion, and the suspect ran away heading west.

The suspect is believed to be in her 40's. She has long brown hair with reddish tints, was wearing a tank top, shorts, and sunglasses.

McNeil said the mother was using the restroom in the back of the business when the child's screaming started."

KY3- TV News 2013

The little 6-year-old girl was left alone at a table in the fast food restaurant. We might be realizing a much different scenario had the child not "fell to the floor and began screaming."

A simple, effective message in abduction prevention is to teach our children to do just what this child did. Teach, *"Do not comply, fall to the floor or ground, scream, and do not stop screaming until you know you are safe."*

Notice that the predator was a casually dressed female whose appearance incited no alarm or concern. She was very bold to enter that business and attempt that abduction. We simply have to educate ourselves and our children with Godly boldness. I think we should teach them to scream "Jesus" at full volume.

Should the mother have left the child alone at a table? Probably not, and one suspects she will not again. The predator had to have stalked, waited, and been ready to grab that little girl. She obviously expected no resistance.

The purposed parent teaches and instructs their child. The parent has power of voice and authority. The key is simple: Before the predator strikes, be there with parental purpose, and protective instruction for your child. Get there first.

One popular prevention of abduction is to have a code word with your child to prevent abduction. If the person attempting to take the child does not know the code or confidential word, the child is instructed not to go with the person. That is good up to a point. Please remember, that these predators are skilled in gaining the confidences of children. They are much more cunning than a child. They study ways to break that parental safety code word.

The best prevention is to have one or two safe people on call in case there is an emergency and you cannot pick up the child. It is much more secure to teach, "No one can pick you up but me or (name two other "safe list" people). No one." Simple and more safe.

Clearly, according to Matthew 18, every caring adult is responsible for training children. Obviously, parents are to have and utilize the greatest influence in that training. We have a holy call and purpose to train them, educate them, and embrace them with listening skills, as we help them in their walk with Jesus.

One great table of promised provision and hope is Luke 1:17. *"He will also go before Him in the spirit and power of Elijah, 'to turn the hearts of the fathers to the children, and the disobedient to the wisdom of the just, to make ready a people prepared for the Lord."* The word for *father* in this verse, according to Strong's Concordance denotes the meaning to also be, *"both parents."*

Luke 1:17 is wonderful and good news. Our hearts desire and prayer is that this promise is fulfilled in every reader and shared with all who matter to you.

"My son (or daughter), hear the instruction of your father, And do not forsake the law of your mother;" - Proverbs 1:8

Let us be diligent and delighted in the giving of our instruction and law.

PRAYER: *Father, teach us to teach children. Counsel us in the holy instruction of safety for them. Help us to give them instruction in such a way that they will desire to follow and obey. We want them to always be embraced with our voice and Your loving law. Increase our time and instruct us in the prioritization of time. We praise You that we have time for our children. We praise You for Your daily wisdom in achieving success in every facet of our lives. Thank You for families in the home, our extended family, and in Your church who all work together for children, the innocent and the greatest in Your kingdom. We call children into our midst as we imitate You and respond joyfully and successfully to Your Word. In Jesus Name, let us instruct and teach the Word and the law of protection to Your children. Amen.*

Z is for ZEALOUS

John 10:10 is a contest scripture. We see that Jesus came because He desires to give us His Life and abundant way of living. The "thief" that is the devil, has a threefold objective. He determines to *"steal, kill, and destroy"* God's life in us.

Let us unfold the enemy strategy for clarity and trustingly to prevent his corruption.

- he manipulates to *"steal"* our identity.
- he then *"kills"* by altering our passion.
- he then is positioned to *"destroy"* our purpose.

In this section we will look at his plot for killing passion. Please read "I is for Identity" and "Y is for Your Purpose" for amplification of "steal and destroy".

Zeal is defined as *"great energy or enthusiasm in pursuit of a cause or an objective"; and as "one burning with zeal, most eagerly desirous, vehemently contending for a thing". It is "an intense desire or enthusiasm for something, passion, It is eagerness, fire, animation, spirit, vigor."*

Strong's Concordance; New American Oxford Dictionary

This is a vital word. It is in the definition and understanding of this word that we see why the enemy has focused determination to "kill" our God given passion, our fire, our zeal.

The antonym of passion is revealing. One opposite word is "apathy". This is a word that denotes a lot of lack: lack of interest, lack of concern, lack of response, etc... It expresses indifference and impassivity. It denotes depression and bleakness of soul. A lack of passion is a lack of motion. People are created by God to be motivated, that is stimulated, energized, enthusiastically moved, by passion.

The devil hates, really hates, people who have passion (zeal) for God and the ways and plans of God. He hates that we are to have enthusiasm and great energy in our God given life.

If the devil steals your identity then his next step is to kill your passion. If we do not know that we belong to God, and that we are to imitate Him as His own dear children, then the enemy has stolen our identity. Without an identity, our passion is easy prey for the devil and his minions.

"Our God is a consuming fire." We need His fire as our motivation to achieve. Indeed, He "baptizes us with The Holy Spirit and with fire." God is a zealous, consuming fire, and we need His fire. It is our motivation, our passion to achieve and live life to the fullest and to have the "vigor and eagerness" to help others to realize the same. (Hebrews 12:29; Matthew 3:11)

The devil cannot always extinguish the fire, passion, zeal of God, so he appropriates it and causes abuse with it. Make no mistake about it, he wants God's fire. We can see this in action in King David's life.

Read II Samuel 11:1-14

The first thing we see is the stealing of David's Identity as King. Kings were supposed to be off to the place of battle. King David, probably because of pride of life, did not go. He was on the roof.

And there he sees Bathsheba, lusts with his eyes, and directs his passion toward her. David's zeal, passion, for God, by his flesh responding to the enemy, became a tool of the enemy. His passion for God was killed, redirected to himself and his lust. He who had been used as an instrument of worship and leadership, became in effect, "strange fire."

Then King David goes on to operate in his flesh-lust, to connive, to betray, to lie, and to murder, destroy, his own people. He became, temporarily, like the father of lies who was a murderer from the beginning.

David was not a child molester. But the principles of rebellion apply and his irresponsible and flesh actions resulted in the death of a child, his child. (2 Samuel 12:18)

David did what sex offenders often do. He "fixated", that is, he *"developed an obsessive attachment to an object"* (New American Oxford Dictionary). His obsession was with his own flesh desires and Bathsheba was merely the "object" of his lust. We know from this written truth that nothing that had once been valued by David, stood in the way of this obsession. He lost reason, perspective, and his Godly character. He was not a child sex offender and he did authentically repent. The principles of this story however, teach the power of flesh and the path of rebellion. A child sex offender is a person propelled by flesh and rebellion.

Fixations can develop on Facebook, or other avenues our children's images are placed. Please exercise caution before giving or posting information of any kind regarding your child; home address, school address, name of family pets, shirts with their school logos, etc. We live in these cautionary times. Reread David's story and think about how a person of his caliber became such a tool of the enemy.

It can even happen on an outing in "real life" as one parent is well aware. This parent noticed a male individual pointing his phone camera at his attractive daughter. The alert parent immediately photographed the suspicious male and said, *"I now have your picture."* The possible predator fled. We are not to fear but, we must be wise and alert.

David did not in this depiction win the contest of John 10:10. Of course the enemy also utilized his weaponry: (1 John 2:16)

- the pride of life (I'll go where I want)
- lust of the eyes (I see it- I want it- I will have it)
- and lust of the flesh (whoever gets in the way of "me" must be eliminated)

This sounds like the devil and every sex offender we have encountered or read about.

The zeal, the fire of God must not be quenched or redirected by our enemy; he wants us passionless about our children. If he cannot put out the fire he will attempt to redirect it toward a flesh centered matter.

Zeal as it relates to God is defined as a vigorous and fierce show of protection for those who belong to Him (Strong's Concordance). We are to be zealous for children under our protection as well. He has placed us to provide a safe place for the innocents. May that zeal consume us.

"Thus says the Lord of hosts: "I am zealous for Zion with great zeal; With great fervor I am zealous for her." - Zechariah 8:2

The zeal of God does not fade, alter, or waiver. He is constant in His burning passion for us. And He will reignite us simply by our asking Him to do so.

God, our God, burns with fervor over His Creation, over what belongs to Him. There is nothing casual or dismissive about our Lord.

138

Questions to ponder:

1. Is there a better work than guarding God's children and "burning with a zeal", His zeal, to do so?
2. Is fighting for and defending the innocence of a child worth the energy of your fire?
3. Has the enemy stolen your identity as a defender of children?
4. Has your fire been lacking or redirected by the enemy toward things that are not Kingdom business?
5. Are you by selfishness allowing or even participating in the destroying of God's little ones?

These are huge questions.

Let us determine to identify and stand in the place of Kingdom business. Let us determine to yield to God's Fire and Passion that sheds Light on enemy tactics and burns away demonic plans. Let us destroy the enemy strongholds and build the Kingdom of Heaven.

"Behold, children are a heritage from the Lord, the fruit of the womb is a reward."   - Psalm 127:3

His heritage. Lord, we ask and receive a fresh infilling of the Holy Spirit and Fire as we delight to do your will.

PRAYER: *Father, we ask that You ignite us to passionately pursue Your plan for Your children. Show us what we am purposed to do. We pray that the eyes of our understanding be enlightened and that we may know the hope of Your calling. Teach us Your way, O Lord, we will walk in Your Truth, unite our heart to fear Your Name. May our lives give You glory in all the ways that matter to You. Like You, we hate the destruction of children by abortion, molestation, abduction, and all the atrocities that the devil has devised. We will walk in Your authority and power. We praise You for answers, solutions, and ultimate Life and triumph for Your Body. God bless Your children through us and help us to teach others to ignite as well. Praise You, Abba Father for Your Fire in us. We burn with desire to guard children and to be a defender of the innocent, In Jesus Name. Amen."*

No One is Born a Pedophile
By Dr. Keith Ablow
Published November 28, 2012
FoxNews.com

A recent article on Gawker.com by Cord Jefferson suggests that we could be a more just and healing society were we to consider pedophilia a sexual orientation, rather than simply a crime. He suggests that pedophiles are born with this orientation, just as men might be born with the inherent potential to develop an attraction to adult females, or vice-versa.

Here, Jefferson promotes a predictable (because it has been said before) and extremely dangerous claim that wanting to have sex with kids means nothing psychologically about the person who wants to. Further, it suggests that when one cannot resist having sex with a child that that person is a victim of mental illness beyond his or her control, which he or she has no responsibility to resist.

The truth is that no one has ever been able to demonstrate that a person is born destined - genetically or neurologically - to want to have sex with children. The evidence for differences in the brains of pedophiles and those attracted to adults could easily be accounted for by traumatic life experiences of a sexual nature. We already know that trauma changes the brain. Life experience influences the function and structure of the nervous system. Pedophiles, while worthy of pity because they are in fact sick, aren't born, in my opinion.

Sadly, pedophiles who won't accept responsibility for their actions may be inappropriately seeking to "benefit" from the advances won by the gay rights movement, because that movement has asserted that homosexual behavior is pre-programmed into babies, just as heterosexual behavior is. The unscientific and rote intolerance on the part of some gay rights groups for the idea that life experience can also shape sexual orientation (that sexual orientation is fluid) plants the seeds for the same insistence by those who would prey upon children.

I have treated many people with sexual disorders, including pedophilia. Not one of them was without extremely significant childhood trauma. I defy any mental health professional to introduce me to a pedophile whose early life experiences did not include inappropriate boundary crossings and failure of empathy by adults around that person- whether sexually violent or otherwise humiliating.

Pedophiles, while worthy of pity because they are in fact sick, aren't born, in my opinion. They are made by traumatic life experiences. Moreover, even once they are created, many resist their impulses because they understand what should be - but is not - obvious to all of them: Forcing oneself on a child, through assault or coercion is morally abhorrent and illegal.

Resisting sexual impulses is a very common occurrence. It happens billions of times a day on the planet. Married people do it routinely, even though they are attracted to other partners.

People who would like to be Peeping Toms because they are sexually attracted by voyeurism routinely resist acting on their desires because they understand them to be morally and legally wrong.

Teachers attracted to teenage students routinely resist cavorting with them because they would lose their jobs and because it is wrong to indulge.

People who might be excited by hiring prostitutes often resist because they understand that consummating the relationship would be breaking the law or because they intuit that buying sex from a young woman could be doing her psychological harm, even if she insists otherwise.

People attracted to their best friend's girlfriends routinely resist because they understand that consummating the relationship would be wrong.

Those who do not resist pedophilic desires - and who actually have sexual contact with a child (not simply looking at sexual images online, by the way, which is a matter for another column) - have made a choice. That choice is reprehensible and legally indefensible.

No one must have sex with a child. No one is born, in fact, absolutely needing to. No evidence exists, whatsoever, that the brain at birth is different in pedophiles than in the rest of the population. And treatments do exist that can dramatically reduce pedophilic impulses - including the use of Depo-Provers injections which tank testosterone levels.

The elevation of pedophilia to sexual orientation clears the way for more of it. And Cord Jefferson conspires with that potential in his writings.

Dr. Ablow's articles are printed by permission from his office (Amy).
Appreciation and prayers to Dr. Ablow.